student and graduate praise for
first job ~ first paycheck

"College students will actually want to read this fun and informational book. It will be a great resource long after you graduate."
- Kimi G, student @ University of Washington

"The real deal that is to-the-point, and informative - all while keeping my attention." *- LeCory R, University of Central Florida, now a MBA candidate @ Texas A&M - Commerce*

"A frank, informative and entertaining look at what it means to take responsibility for one's success – financially and otherwise."
- John W, student @ University of San Francisco

"An informative and enjoyable read. It answered my questions and has already helped me head in the right direction."
- Jason C, student @ University of Washington

"A practical, common sense guide to personal finance for every college student…it should be required reading."
- Philip K, MBA student @ University of Central Florida

"A 'straight-shooter' approach to understanding professional and personal goals. Thanks for the lessons – I will carry them with me throughout my life." *- Paul J, student @ University of San Francisco*

"Incredible book. Great advice that should definitely be learned before graduating college." *- Jessica P, University of Central Florida, BMG Models, now a MBA candidate @ Texas A&M - Commerce*

"A very informative book that provides information that is far from common sense. I wish it had been integrated into my college curriculum." *- Adrian S, Columbia University, now @ Google*

"This book challenges you to think differently and will help you avoid common mistakes that others will make."
- Craig G, University of Central Florida, student @ Rollins College and now @ Darden Corp

student and graduate praise for
first job ~ first paycheck

"A great book that is refreshing and motivating. It opened my eyes to a lot of information that I would have never seen. I'm telling all my friends about it."
- George J, University of Washington,
now a professional soccer player @ FC Dallas

"I have a lot better perspective on things after reading this book. It is honest and straightforward. If it existed when I was in school I would definitely be even better off now."
- Jimmy T, University of Central Florida,
now @ Cox Media

"Contains valuable insight that is not available in the classroom. Highlights the steps to take now that will lead to large gains in the future."
- Khynna B, University of Washington,
now @ Sun Life Financial

"I definitely have a more educated perspective on my financial and professional priorities as a result of reading this book."
- Chase H, Columbia University, now @ Google

"Covers just about every challenge you will have coming out of college. It's a great compilation of starting points and check-ins on the road to success."
- Evan T, University of Washington, now @ MyBinding

"Read this book while you are in school and after you get your first job...the info is priceless and can put you ahead of the game. It will talk you out of doing things you will regret financially."
- Tyler W, University of Central Florida,
formerly @ Kavaliro, now @ Millennium Laboratories

"This book will provide you with answers to your questions: The ones you wanted to ask, the ones you didn't want to ask, and those that you didn't know you should ask. I only wish it was available a year ago!"
- Kaitie F, University of Washington,
now @ a major wine distributor

"This book is one-of-a-kind. An informative, honest and quick read that does an excellent job of preparing you for the real world."
- Bridget B, University of Central Florida,
now @ Millennium Laboratories

student and graduate praise for
first job ~ first paycheck

"Regardless of your major this book is engaging, enjoyable, practical and a must read. There's lots of actionable advice to get you started on the path to professional success and financial freedom."

- David B, University of Central Florida,
Co-Founder @ Group Table and CEO @ Brand Advance

"A quick read that's concise, thorough and more helpful than six multi-topic financial planning books. It's filled with straight facts, zero fluff and is immediately applicable."

- Kelley F, University of Washington, Amazon.com,
now @ Northwest Group Real Estate

"An eye-opener of a book that will cause you to re-evaluate your career decisions and overall life goals. It is one book that you will keep referring back to again and again."

- Natalie E, University of Central Florida,
now @ evok advertising

"A must-read for any college student who needs guidance on landing a job, managing your money and preparing for your future. If you want a financially secure future read this book."

- Britnee W, University of Washington,
now @ Vistakon (Johnson & Johnson)

"Provides knowledge that you would not normally pick up as a college student. Gives you information you would usually have to learn from making mistakes."

- Eric K, University of Central Florida, now @ Google

"The tips and insights are not only spot-on, they're actionable and presented in a way that is incredibly easy to understand. This book really blew me away. You'll want to pick it up again and again."

- Edison C, University of Central Florida,
formerly @ Facebook.com, now @ Playfish (Electronic Arts)

"This book has given me a clear understanding on how to have fun growing my money! I found myself highlighting various points to help allocate them to memory, just like in college."

- Andrew G, University of Central Florida,
now @ IKON Office Solutions, Inc. (A Ricoh Company)

first job
first paycheck
how to get the most out of both
...without help from your parents

JEFF LEHMAN

MENTOR
PRESS LLC
Seattle WA

first job ~ first paycheck

how to get the most out of both
...without help from your parents

Copyright © 2011, 2016 MENTOR PRESS LLC

ISBN13: 978-0-9768999-6-9 (Paperback)
ISBN/ASIN: 0976899965

ISBN13: 978-0-9768999-3-8 (eBook)
ISBN/ASIN: 0976899930

Library of Congress Control Number: 2011901957

First Edition, Second Printing
Printed in the United States of America

Quantities of this book are available at a volume discount.
For more information, please contact us at:
www.FirstJobFirstPaycheck.com
www.facebook.com/FirstJobFirstPaycheck

MENTOR
PRESS LLC
Seattle WA

To those who have helped me,
shown me how to help others,
or who have asked for my help.

Thank You

CONTENTS

Disclaimer

The information in this book is provided to get you thinking about how to get the most out of your first job and first paycheck. Ultimately, it is your choice to make and this book initiates that discussion. I am not a career counselor or financial advisor. Before making any career or financial decisions always talk to someone who is neutral and knowledgeable about these topics, and whose professional opinion you trust. I call them mentors. Make sure they don't have a vested interest in profiting from any of the decisions you make. It's your future, so choose wisely. And, good luck!

INTRODUCTION

~

Welcome to the real world!

Have you ever had one of those moments where the person right next to you comes up with a really great idea...one that you'd never heard of before? You find yourself thinking: "I wish I had thought of that. I'm smart, so why didn't I?" Then you have this momentary feeling of sitting still and being left behind by a big crowd of people who are moving forward to future successes? You feel queasy and upset...like you are about to lose out on a big opportunity.

What's up with that?

I found myself wondering this when I was in college. I wanted to be the one who was coming up with new ideas and solving problems. I wanted to be respected for my creativity before I got out into the real world. Then I figured out the secret to it all. I realized that I was the only one who could make things happen in my life. No one was going to hand anything to me. I had to apply myself 110%.

So what did I do?

I got actively involved in everything I could. I shared ideas with people. I listened. I became a more critical thinker. I started applying what I was being taught. I learned outside of my class curriculum requirements. I took the classes from the hardest professors. I made friends with those professors. I did all I could to excel in college. I took on extra responsibilities whenever I could. Long story short: I got fully engaged in life. Then the ideas started coming to me, and that has helped me tremendously in the workplace.

I also did everything I legally could to fully live my life. I was willing to try new projects, even if I failed. And many times I did fail. I tried to stay away from the negative people who said: "We've always done it this way." I wanted to find a new path to getting things done smarter while using as much of my brain as possible. I thought that

1

there always had to be a better way to do things. Otherwise there would be no such thing as entrepreneurs and start-ups.

Along this path I learned a lot and became successful. I'm still learning every day, and I still don't always get it right. Now it's time to share with you some of what I've learned. This is an important point in your life. The decisions you make now will have a big effect on your future. I want to provide you with some of those really great ideas that very few others around you are thinking about right now. This book can open your eyes to a lot of things you haven't had the time to consider. And, maybe it will help you to start developing your own great ideas on how to succeed in life.

Now is the best time in your life to re-think all those *often-repeated myths* about life, work and money that you've heard over and over again from people of all ages. I will talk about these in the pages ahead. It's time to get creative and find new ways to think about what matters most to you. The great thing about being young is that you haven't had a chance to screw up too much yet, hopefully nothing(!), right? So, why not get started in life with a mentor who will show you how to think smarter the first time around?

Where will you go to get your personal finance advice?

This book is about how to get the most out of your first job and your first paycheck. The emphasis is mostly on the paycheck part. You are probably wondering who was going to be helping you out with these aspects of your life.

In mid-2010 CareerBuilder.com reported that 77% of the working population was living paycheck-to-paycheck. Also in mid-2010 almost 10% of the population was unemployed. That means that 87% of the population that could be bringing home a paycheck wasn't in a position to save money and accumulate wealth. And, not everyone who was employed in 2010 (and wasn't living paycheck-to-paycheck) had their financial act together either. The economy has gotten a little better as I write this, but do the math anyway - most people today are getting their financial "advice" from people who aren't truly the best source for it. Did you go to college so you could ultimately end up living paycheck-to-paycheck like so many people around you? I didn't think so.

Want more proof that most people aren't savvy with their money? To help promote my second book, *The Frugal Millionaires*, I launched TheFrugalTest.com. Visitors to that site are invited to take a 25 question multiple-choice test that measures their overall frugal aptitude. No personal information is gathered and the test takes less than 10 minutes. Over 6,000 people have taken it so far. Out of 100 possible points the average score is consistently 63. FAIL! So, before you take any financial advice from adults consider having them take the test first. If they score 90 or higher some of their ideas *might* be worth considering, but only if those ideas fit into *your* personal financial plans.

Personally, I've always looked to super successful people with solid financial plans and a high net worth to get valuable advice. And I'm not talking about the ones who have inherited their money or gotten rich writing books about getting rich. Only about 2% of our population is millionaires, so there aren't that many "money experts" to choose from. And not all millionaires have their financial act together either. The truly wise ones are hard to find. You'll see towards the end of the book that I found many of them. Their advice can help you.

This book is a catalyst to help you, if you are willing to consider some new ideas about jobs *and* money. My goal is to be the one giving you the great ideas that no one else is thinking about so they can be used to your advantage. These ideas have already been creating great careers and wealth for people just like you. There are no short cuts though; if you want to be successful you'll have to work for it. No one is going to hand it to you. This book can give you a competitive edge on getting what you want in life.

I have felt what you are feeling now.

When I was a senior in college, I wish someone had handed me a book like this. That's why I wrote it. I might have been better at getting more out of my first job and first paycheck. Still, I managed to piece it all together on my own and make smart choices. You now have easier access to ideas that can help you right now.

You are graduating at a pivotal time in the history of our country. As someone who is new to the workforce you are in a better position to take advantage of the coming economic upswings than any generation since the Great Depression. When I graduated college the economy was also in the midst of a recession. I can relate to what you are going through, but it's different this time. It's been worse, but it's getting better now.

The good news is that today you have more access to information and tools that can make you smarter about work and money than ever before. You just have to be resourceful enough to use them. One thing I've learned in life is if you don't take care of your career and money, someone else will try to...and you probably won't like the results.

You can learn life lessons from the strangest situations.

Years ago I was on hiatus from work and training for a transatlantic yacht race. I met a racing skipper from the UK who was on break from a grueling around-the-world yacht race. His boat was being retrofitted before heading into the gale-force winds of the treacherous Southern Ocean. He was visiting a long time friend in San Francisco who happened to be my training skipper. At a crew dinner I asked him if he knew what he was going to do after his big race ended in just six months. He said:

> *"Mate, you always need to know what you're doing next,*
> *before you step off the boat."*

That was an excellent thought. It was another one of those: "Why didn't I think of it that way?" moments. Sometimes your life lessons come from unexpected encounters. Before you step off the graduation podium and into your first job and first paycheck you should know what you're going to be doing with both.

After you have graduated a lot of your world centers around your life, your job, your career and what you do with the money you make. You go from the broad focus of college and lots of like-minded people to the narrow focus of your very specific life. You might wonder: Why will some of your classmates be professionally successful while others won't? Why will some be wealthy and others won't? The choices we make early in life can greatly affect the outcome of our lives on many levels over the years. It's not something we're inclined to think about at a young age, but we should. Those who do will benefit greatly. You are the skipper of your own life now.

Why write a book if you don't need the money?

The inspiration to write this book came from mentoring hundreds of college students and guest lecturing to thousands more. We have learned from each other. I have never turned down a student who wanted to be mentored...but the word is out now and I can't get to everyone personally so this book is the next best thing. Maybe it's even better...it will always be accessible to you.

Giving back is important to me. I don't want to be remembered for having made a bunch of money (not that anyone will care). I'd rather be remembered for helping you.

In the pages ahead you'll be exposed to a lot of ideas that many of your fellow graduates might never begin to ponder. If you put them to good use you'll be richer for it in many ways. There's plenty of money to go around in this world if you are smart enough to find and manage it.

One thing you should know, and this is important to me: You won't find any attempts in this book to sell you anything that I benefit from personally. I do suggest in the book that you purchase a few things, but I have no affiliation with those companies or any other sources I mention in this book. The only vested interest I have is that you get something out of what you read and use the resources I've provided. And, as I have done with the other books I've written, the profits from this one will be used to cover modest expenses, continue to "give back," and make donations to selected charities.

You can be successful in your first job and with your first paycheck, and you will be able to do it all on your own, with help from this book. Enjoy *First Job ~ First Paycheck*. Make these ideas your own and go out and make a difference in the real world.

Jeff Lehman
Seattle, WA

SECTION I:
Getting your first job

Chapter 1
~

Why your best career is in
a market that doesn't exist yet

Smart, creative, entrepreneurial people color outside the lines.
They also create new types of boxes to put the color into.

When I started looking for my first job the economy was in a recession. Does that sound familiar? I had to move to the other side of the country to find employment. I just looked at it like it was a big adventure. It was, and it still is.

If I made any mistakes in that early job search it was that I was looking at traditional jobs in traditional market segments. You know, the markets where the jobs disappear first in a recession! I had to look extra hard to find any company that was hiring. I didn't know any better. I still got a good job and started to learn what it was like in the real world of paying my own bills and being responsible for my own actions.

Once that recession ended so did my connection with the traditional job market. I finally figured it out:

It's more fun making new rules than living by the old ones.

However, many people never figure this out because, according to one recent graduate: "The upbringing and education of many people sets them up for a pre-programmed path in life, and that loss of creativity and adventure is awful!"

It's always good to be focused on the *next* new thing when it comes to plotting your career. That's where career success and tremendous financial upside exists. If you can get a job with a company in the emerging market segments that I've outlined in the next chapter (or others) you'll potentially be that much more ahead in the career game.

> GO WHERE THE SMART MONEY IS GOING: Want to know where the hot emerging grow categories might be? Look at where angel investors and venture capitalists are putting their money right now. Start by looking for the angels and VCs in your local area. For more information type these phrases into your favorite search engine: *"angel investors + your city,"* or try *"venture capitalists + your city."* Take a look at their websites and see what types of investments they are making. All the sites are different so you'll have to do a little digging. It's worth it.

Use the same process above to look at major cities around the country where you might want to live and see if you can find a repeating pattern of market segments that the smart money is chasing.

Once you find a market segment that's interesting to you, narrow your focus down to the companies within that segment. Look at these companies as if you were investing your hard earned life savings in them. In a sense you are investing your soon-to-be-future earning potential in them.

Do what you need to do to get into these companies: informational interviews, alumni connections, cold calls, internships, job interviews, etc. Once you get into these companies don't be over-sold by the recruiters...they are paid to get you excited. Do as much of your own research as you think is necessary to convince yourself the company is for you.

This is where it's good to have a great mentor (there will be more on this later in the book). Ask them what they think about the products or services of your potential employer. A good mentor will tell you straight up what they think. Ask them to be completely honest about any jobs you are considering. Have a few mentors for balance...and pick those that have a forward-looking perspective.

Look at your potential employer's financial statements and analyst reports, if available. Look at who runs the company and what other companies they worked for. That info is usually buried on their website somewhere in the "about us" section. Determine if you have any connections to them. Leverage those connections. Also read industry trade websites, magazines and newspapers to see what is really going on in that market segment.

When it comes down to making an employment choice consider this: What could be the difference between working for Twitter, Groupon, Friendster, LinkedIn, MySpace or Facebook? They all seem similar in their potential, right? Or they did at some point early in their development. Their differences may not seem like much until one or two of the companies take off, become highly successful, and go public or get acquired while the others do not. Choose wisely and be your own best critic when it comes to picking a company to work for.

As you plan your career, keep an open mind towards going where the action is. Some people never leave the town they grew up in, or the one they were educated in, because they have friends and family there, or they are comfortable with a status quo life that has no surprises. That's becoming less and less the norm for successful people these days...especially Millennials. Push past your comfort zone and you'll be in a position to excel in ways that you never thought possible.

Chapter 2

~

Recession-proofing your career

We are slowly exiting the Great Recession, the worst one most of us will ever know. Many people working for traditional companies felt the pain, like: General Motors, Chrysler, AT&T, Qwest, Time Warner, Motorola, Clearwire, Washington Mutual (gone!), Lehman Brothers (gone! - and I'm not related to them) and Countrywide Mortgage (gone!). Many of these companies are still here and now recovering. The ones that are no longer with us are gone for many reasons. Some were unethical, some made bad strategic business decisions, and others were crushed under their debt and expense structures. Lessons have been learned and new opportunities have been created.

Many people who worked at Google, Facebook, LinkedIn, Apple, Audi, BMW, Netflix, Amazon, Southwest Airlines, Ford, Redbox, Twitter, Groupon, Verizon, Zynga and Cisco felt minimal or no pain. Recession? What recession? OK, maybe they did feel it a little – but who didn't? What made it different for them? Simply put, these companies had unique or next generation products and services that people still wanted even when times were tough. Many had great brands and were well-managed. Or, they had a fantastic new idea that capitalized on a market opportunity and created a whole new product category. People who worked for these companies had essentially "recession proofed" their careers, whether they knew it or not. They probably did.

You want to be working in the "new" markets.

What exactly is a recession proof career? It's finding a company in an existing or emerging growth market that provides new and innovative products and services that people find value in. Early in my career it was the personal computer market and then the Internet market. *They didn't exist when I was in college.* Let me repeat that: *They didn't exist when I was in college.*

That's a key point. It's now hard to think of not having either in our lives, but that wasn't always the case. They have almost become traditional markets...except that many of the companies in this segment have found new innovations that have surpassed their original business models. And newer companies have emerged with even fresher ideas.

Emerging growth markets to consider might include:

- Clean energy (solar/wind/water)
- Gas, Oil & Natural Gas
- Home energy storage and resale
- Green building *(the cost effective version)*
- Entrepreneurial/start-up services
- Online and/or mobile bill pay services
- Consumer Internet
- Cloud computing services
- Social networking games/applications
- Group driven discount networks
- Next generation social networks
- Cost efficient, sustainability/recycling
        products and services
- Electric/hybrid transportation
- Preventive health care
- Modern green pre-fab compact housing
- Space efficient architectural design
- Obesity / diabetes management
- Commercial software and services
- Mobile communication devices
- Mobile advertising
- Digital media and advertising
- Search engine / Social media marketing
- Next generation Internet web services

- Tablet computing
- Bison ranching *(no, I'm not kidding)*
- Space tourism *(OK, maybe I am kidding here...
    but who knows?)*
- Life sciences - biotech, biochemistry,
    bio-engineering, ecology, smart
    biopolymers, nanotechnology, etc.
- Networking and IT infrastructure
- Computer gaming *(maybe)*
- Medical informatics
- Low-energy consumption products
- Tankless water heaters
- Geothermal heat pumps
- Energy efficient climate control
- 4G, 5G, 6G, etc. - any next generation wireless
- Doing business with China, South Korea
    and India
- Infrastructure rebuilding in Japan
- Ethical financial planning and investing
- Ethical accelerated mortgage repayment
    services
- Anything else *ethical...*

There are many more but these should get you thinking. There are also many traditional jobs that support the emerging markets like: advertising, legal, business consulting, accounting, etc. If you can align yourself in some way with an emerging market you will have the potential for more upside in your career.

Additionally, some new opportunities will emerge from within the more "traditional" market segments as companies innovate to stay ahead.

*There is opportunity everywhere if you are
creative enough to see it and go after it.*

HOW DO YOU GET INTO THESE MARKETS?

First word: *Resourcefulness*

You have to seek out these markets and the companies in them. How do you find out about them? In addition to the tips that I gave you in the first chapter of this section it's best to have a solid reading list that keeps you updated in the emerging markets where you have interest. I recommend business, special interest and trade media because it is more detailed in its coverage and you see it there first, before it hits the mainstream media networks. Sign-up for the online versions of newspapers and magazines that cover the market segments you are interested in. Try to get the print versions at your local library as well. They will be more complete. Also browse news releases on PRNewswire.com. This is where the news happens before you see it in the typical media.

Read all your sources constantly, it is amazing how often you can be the first one to connect with a new opportunity if you stay on top of things.

Second word: *Internship*

When you see companies that you are interested in, get in contact with them. Find out who is in charge of internships and approach them.

In emerging markets there is a "problem" that creates opportunities for you. The problem is money. In start-ups there is very little of it to hire a big staff of expensive, well-seasoned people. Many people older than you have a lot of bills to pay, they have spouses and families so they don't typically look for jobs with start-ups. These jobs are also often viewed as too risky. Interning for a brief period, like a quarter or semester, puts you in a good position for a full time job when you graduate.

REAL LIFE IDEAS: Let's say that you can't get the internship that you want. A recent graduate who I mentored has gone on to start two successful companies. He's quite the entrepreneur and suggests that: "If you can't find that perfect internship you should *build your own* by starting a venture or creating a business service offering in your field." You can add to that by creating your own blog on your field of interest, attending industry related events, and volunteering - all so that you stay current.

That recent graduate also offered these additional thoughts: "Many students get stuck working in a job that isn't in their field. What will happen in the years ahead when the economy turns around and companies start hiring again? They will most likely hire someone with experience who lost their job, or a new college grad with more recent exposure to the field. If you have not been making advancements in your field, keeping up with your skills, etc., what value proposition do you have to offer a potential employer? At least if you have a small company or pet project you can show them your ambition, vision and potential."

START YOUR OWN LLC: Did you know that in most states you can create your own Limited Liability Corporation (LLC) for around $100-$200? Creating a LLC is fairly straightforward. So why not do it? Type: "*create an LLC in (your state)*" into your favorite search engine for more information.

HOT TIPS FROM ANOTHER RECENT GRADUATE:

1. Online Job Boards: If there is a company that really interests you bookmark their online job board site and check it constantly. Check it as often as you check your Facebook page each day (or more, if that's humanly possible). That could be the winning strategy. You might be able to pick-off an internship or a job before anyone else sees it. This exact strategy helped a recent graduate score an internship with a major technology company.

2. Resource Centers: Most universities have a resource center. Do you know where yours is? Become best friends with the staff there and see if they can help place you in an internship or job. Some universities also have co-op programs in place. Do you know how to find out about them? As a recent graduate points out: "Students often assume that if they don't know about it, it doesn't exist. I found an incredible opportunity at my university's experiential learning center and had virtually no competition for the position. No one really knew about their internship placement service."

3. Strategic Geography: Find an address for a major building in a city where you are interested in interning (think of the biggest most prestigious business address in the town you are interested in, that isn't occupied by one company). Then use Google Maps to locate it. Type: *"businesses at (that address and city)"* and see what pops up. Then go through the list and cold-call the companies and ask if they are looking for interns. A recent graduate who did this got 3 great leads, including an internship offer, in the first 5 search results.

Third word: *Resume*

Having an internship with an innovative start-up can add real firepower to your resume. It can position you as being entrepreneurial, fearless, and high energy. These are all things that can differentiate you in a competitive job setting. Your resume doesn't have to "look" any different than others...but it does need to "read" different. It's the content (your experiences) that will make you stand apart from the others.

Chapter 3

~

World's easiest resume

Resumes aren't as complicated as everyone makes them out to be...at least not any longer. You don't need an expensive book or consultant to tell you how to make one. Take the simple resume approach that over 100,000,000 people use...its called LinkedIn, a business oriented social network. If you choose to join LinkedIn (it's free at linkedin.com) you put all your career data in and the onscreen profile version of your resume is right there for you.

By using a ubiquitous resume format that others already use your resume is less likely to be rejected for any of the cutesy stuff that some people typically use to differentiate themselves (and that recruiters and HR people dislike – and dislike is a kind word here).

Here are the basic components of a LinkedIn online profile:

- Name
- Current position
- Location
- Any new/updated information
    (that you think is important)
- Past
    (previous positions held)
- Education

A more in-depth version follows the last set of components:

- Summary
    (of your career)

- Specialties
    (the kind of work you are really good at)
- Experience
    (includes job titles, employment dates, brief description of what you did and web site contact info – these are listed in chronological order with the most recent listed at the top)
- Education
    (also chronological – university you attended, degree you obtained, dates you attended, summary of what you studied, activities and societies you were involved in)
- Recommendations
- Additional Info
    (personal business websites, interests, groups you are a part of, and honors and awards)
- Personal information
    (phone, address, IM, birthday, marital status)
    NOTE: Some of this more personal info doesn't need to be on your "paper" resume.

LinkedIn allows you to print a copy of the online version of your resume or download and print a summary version of your resume as an Adobe PDF.

The online version prints fairly small and has a lot more data than the PDF version. The PDF version is different than the onscreen version; it uses a different font and font size.

The PDF version contains the following data:

- Name
- Current title
- E-mail address
- Summary
    (you can use this to discuss what you do, how you do it, what you bring to the table, etc.)

- Experience
    (think "achievements," instead
    of "duties performed")
- Education
- Honors & Awards
- Interests
- Recommendations

The PDF version is better looking than the online version. If you don't like the typeface of the PDF version you can always copy, paste, re-edit it in a word processor and recreate another PDF for your own use. All the flow and formatting work has been done for you, so all you do is make some minimal changes. Easy.

Print a copy of each version and see what you think.

CREATING A GOAL STATEMENT HEADER: I would *highly recommend* that you write out a brief statement about your career goals at the top of your resume (under your name and any basic contact information). The statement can be a combination of the kind of job that you are looking for and how you can help a company achieve their corporate goals. This will go a long way to impress your future employers.

You might also choose to *not* add this feature to your resume so that it has broader appeal inside a larger company. When in doubt, create two resumes.

Chapter 4

~

Networking

In a tough job market you have to stand out. And like I've said, it won't be by putting cutesy stuff on your resume and spamming people with it. It will be by making memorable face-to-face or voice-to-voice contact with professionals in your area of interest.

There are many ways you can meet them:

- Join the local branch of the professional organization that is in your industry.
- Attend professional and alumni networking events.
- Volunteer for industry events and committees.
- Create your own networking group on Facebook. Invite other professionals to join it.
- Establish a blog on the subject and invite industry people in your local area to do guest columns on it.
- Create a "Young _____ Club" in your area. (Pick a category: Sales Executives, Electrical Engineers, Rocket Scientists, CEOs, Nuclear Archeologists, Artists, etc.)
- If you are new to an area see if the local university has a professional organization that you could somehow associate with.
- Track down the departmental assistant in the companies you are interested in and ask what kind of professional organizations their team belongs to. Join those groups.

Your goal is to become an insider.
Insiders get the inside track, and the job.

Networking from the outside can be tough, especially if you are shy and introverted. The cool jobs go to the people who can be resourceful and search them out or even create them on their own. Don't put all your hopes in the hands of company or college recruiters...some things you'll just have to promote on your own behalf.

If you feel that you lack some social skills, go to a few "practice" events to boost your confidence level. These could be local chapters of business associations, alumni organizations, etc. Hit the meeting room hard and make it a goal to meet everyone you possibly can. Size-up quickly how you can help them and how they can help you. The concept of "speed dating" comes to mind here.

> REAL LIFE IDEA: Here's another idea from the recent graduate, who is now an entrepreneur that I mentioned above:

> "A networking tip that I use when trying to connect with someone influential, which I have never heard of anyone using before, is this: If I meet someone at a conference or industry event after talking with them about something relevant and establishing my credibility I ask if I can get a picture with them. A few days later I write them an e-mail reminding them of the conversation and mentioning that it was great to meet them. I then attach the picture to the e-mail and say I thought they'd like a copy. I then have a call to action to possibly connect again and chat more, etc."

> HOT TIPS FROM RECENT GRADUATES: Here are more great ideas from your peers:

> 1. To remember the names of the people you meet when networking make sure you use their name three times in your conversation with them. They will like hearing their name and you'll imprint it on your memory.

2. Make sure you get their business card (and give them yours). Follow-up with a hand written thank-you note initially and a follow-up e-mail at some point after that, as long as you have something to share with them. That shows that you can follow-up and communicate in more than one way.

3. Use LinkedIn as a human professional search engine. It's the most powerful networking tool that one recent graduate has ever found. Search on a market that you are interested in, a geographical location, *and* a group that you share in common, such as a fraternity, sorority or professional organization. You can literally meet new business contacts every week doing this.

The sooner you start the networking process the better off you are. Once you've learned how, it will also help you with job number 2, 3, and 4, etc. Think of it like riding a bike, once you learn you never forget.

Chapter 5

~

Preparing for your interviews

Remember, it's just a conversation.

Interviews are just a conversation that you have with people so they can see if you fit the culture of their company. Realize that you are interviewing "the company" just as much as they are interviewing you. You have to be relaxed and be yourself... just like you are talking with people who you already know and trust. It's like a first date, so have fun.

Here are the typical questions that everyone asks:

- How did you find out about us?
- What do you know about us?
- What value do you think you can add to the company?
- Tell us about your background.
- What type of extracurricular work did you do in college?
- Why should we hire you?
- Did you do any community service projects?
- What are some of your passions?
- What's the worst job experience you've had and tell us how you handled it?
- How have you failed and what did you learn from it?
- How do you like to be managed?
- And my favorite: If you were a tree what kind of tree would you be? (...oh, please!)

Have you heard any of these?

You must be prepared for these questions and have thoughtful and articulate answers. Practice with your friends. You can also go to the web to look up additional sample interview questions and good responses to them. My advice here is to not just memorize answers...but also know enough about yourself to be genuine and forthcoming with what you really think.

Nothing is worse than BS-ing your way into a job
and finding that your new employer
actually expects you to be the way
you portrayed yourself in the interview.

You can also ask questions during the interview process. Smart questions will impress your potential employer.

Here are a few:

- How does the interview/hiring process work at this company?
- What should I prepare for?
- Is it OK to ask questions during the interview process and whom should I ask?
- What qualities do the ideal candidates have?
- Are there people who have been recently hired who I can talk to at some point in the process?
- What makes for a successful employee at this company?

Before you meet with any company for any type of interview do your research. Asking basic questions about the company won't impress your future employer...you should have a base level of knowledge about the company already. Check out their website, research them through your favorite search engine, see what the media is saying and ask around about the company. Maybe an alumnus from your university is there and can give you some information (not *insider* information). Check LinkedIn to see if you have any potential points of contact there. If the company is locally based check out their location. Know what you are walking into before you get there.

There are three important types of interviews you can be involved in: the informational interview, the job interview (there may be many of these with many different people), and the final interview/offer.

1. **Informational Interviews** – Whoever invented these was brilliant. If you are interested in a particular market segment then why not seek out someone who is in the category and ask him or her for a low stress informational interview? I did this early in my career and it changed my life. Others have asked me for informational interviews and I've either hired them or found others who could use their talents. These types of

interviews are very disarming because the expectation level isn't preset to "high."

Use informational interviews as an opportunity to ask a lot of questions. Go as deep on details as the other person will let you. Come to the interview with a list of questions, but be prepared to go into "improvisation mode" if you think of something else to ask.

2. **Job Interviews** – You may have a few of these in the hiring process. As I said earlier, the best approach is to turn them into conversations. The questions should go both ways. No need to be stiff and uncomfortable in the job interview process, its grueling enough already. Being in control of the conversation also helps show confidence. Just be careful not to let your confidence turn into cockiness.

You increase your chances of getting a job by showing that you are a competent communicator and backing that up with a firm knowledge of whatever your area of expertise is. And that's all while remaining humble enough to admit what you don't know, and being willing enough to learn new things. This is very important, and also very difficult. We aren't programmed to admit that we don't know everything – we're college graduates after all! But you are also in your early 20's so how can you possibly know *everything* yet? The truth is that we can never really know everything. Think about it that way instead, it's a more realistic approach...right?

BE CONSISTENT: As you go from interview to interview make sure that you are consistent in your answers. You can be pretty confident that the second you walk out of one person's office and head to the next interview, that the person you just met will be on e-mail or IM telling the interview team what they think. If they didn't like your answer in one interview they may ask you another version of the same question in the next interview. They will be looking for a genuine answer or if you are just telling them what they want to hear.

3. **Final interview/offer** – This is usually when a job offer comes, or is promised. Make sure that you have time to fully consider the offer and ask questions. If you are sure you want the job and the employment package is exactly what you are looking for then go for it before the next person gets a chance. If you need some time ask for 48-72 hours to consider the offer, or ask how long the offer is good for. There are usually many things to consider when you get your first job offer. This is also where your former professors and any current mentors that you have can be extremely helpful.

   If your potential employer wants an immediate decision, and is putting intense pressure on you, chances are there is something they haven't told you or that you haven't uncovered. That's when you should take time to review the offer and make a counter offer if appropriate.

   Always think through as many aspects about the job as you can, including: work load, career path, visibility inside the company, company viability, training programs, competitive forces, uniqueness of product and company, and long term prospects, etc.

   No matter what the case, show your mentor(s) the offer and get their opinion. Once you sign-up for the job you are committed, and only in rare circumstances can you uncommit yourself without ruining your reputation.

What should you wear to an interview?

My advice here is not to guess what you should wear. You'll probably be familiar with what is appropriate in your field, but the easiest way to solve the "what to wear" issue is to ask the person who is walking you through the interview process. They see people coming in for interviews every day and will be your most accurate source of info. The fact that you would ask shows that you care. You'll get a few "style points" for that at least.

Chapter 6

~

16 "must know" interviewing tips

Here are "must know" tips for getting the most out of your interviews and other meetings:

1. **It's just a conversation.** As I've said, remember that you are only having a conversation. This is important when you are trying to learn more about others or the company, and get your key points across. It also helps lower stress.

2. **Watch your "college-isms."** Verbal communications skills are important when you interview and just about any time you converse with others. People in the business world (and adults in general) don't necessary speak or appreciate over-used college-isms such as: well, like, um, cool, you know, uh, ah, and totally, etc. Also avoid being repetitive during a conversation with words like: great, basically, obviously, essentially, fantastic, and awesome, etc.

3. **Have business cards.** Have business/personal cards with you at all times. Make sure you exchange cards with anyone you meet during the interview process.

4. **Show respect.** Show respect by shaking hands firmly and asking for permission to sit down and take notes. Make eye contact and use their name in an appropriate way.

5. Build rapport. Build real rapport by relating to what's in the office of the person you are meeting with. Keep it upbeat, but be careful. You never know if referencing that picture on someone's desk while trying to "relate" to him or her might lead to a long discussion about their imminent divorce from the other person in the picture. Don't waste your time on small talk. Really get to know the other person in a down-to-earth way.

6. Get emotional intelligence. Get some "emotional intelligence" from the other person. How has working for the company enhanced *their* career? What are their aspirations while at the company? Don't go overboard on the personal questions but do take the time to get them know them.

7. Have a goal. Always have a goal for the interview. A good goal might be that they endorse you for the job, endorse you among their peers for the next level of the interview process, give you feedback on how you are doing or open a door to a meeting with someone else. Or better yet, a job offer!

8. Have a fall-back goal. You might not achieve your interview goal (such as getting that job offer) so you need to have an acceptable fallback plan that you can still feel good about. Fallback goals could include any of the goals listed in #7 above.

9. Stay focused. Have a genuine conversation with the other person, but don't be distracted from your goals for the meeting.

10. Know your value proposition. Think about the value that you bring to the table. It's called your "value proposition." What's unique about you? How can you help make things better by being involved with this company? Be able to state it clearly. One recent graduate, who is now a successful businesswoman, had a well thought-out and memorized "3-5 bullet-point" list of her attributes so she could be confident in her answers.

11. Be polite. Since this is an interview, and you are looking for a job, don't be arrogant, condescending or egotistical. Sounds obvious right? I've seen some candidates act like they are doing everyone a favor by showing up to the interview. How would you like that kind of attitude leveled at you?

12. Address objections completely. If the other person expresses a concern about your resume or your answer to a question, say: "If I understand what your concern is..." and then address it. Make sure the issue is handled by asking them, "Did I address your concern?" Then keep the interview moving along.

13. Ask questions. Make sure you are prepared to ask smart questions. Have a few ready and write down any that you come up with during the meeting. Show that you have done your homework on the company and that you are truly interested.

14. Re-cap & commitment. End the interview with a recap of next steps and get a commitment for something significant to both parties and a follow-up meeting if appropriate. Ask the person who interviewed you what the preferred way is to reach them (e-mail, phone, etc.).

15. Ask for the job. When it comes to getting the job, you won't get what you want unless you ask for it.

16. Follow-up promptly. Make sure that you do *sincere* follow-up after the interview using the business card that you got from the other person when you greeted them. That card will help you with the spelling of their name and their correct job title, etc.

Keep practicing your interviewing skills. When it all starts feeling more natural you'll know you are getting there. As another recent graduate, who is now in a successful career, points out: "It's OK to feel uncomfortable with all this at first. By practicing with friends and mentors and doing informational interviews you will get there."

Chapter 7

~

Your social networks are also your unofficial job references

When employers ask for references it's pretty easy to queue up two or three letters of recommendation that say great things about you. References are on the hiring checklist and probably only semi-valuable because...drum roll please...have you ever seen someone submit a reference that has nothing but good comments in it?

With the job market being tighter these days employers need to dig deeper to make sure they are getting the best candidates. There's one job reference that a future employer doesn't need to ask you for...your social network. It can work for or against you. How successful you are depends on how you use these networks to cast you in the proper light.

Many of us have Facebook and LinkedIn profiles. You will probably be asked if you do. Don't think for one minute that they won't be checked - or haven't been already. Not only are your future employers checking to see what information is on your profile that may corroborate or conflict with your resume, they are also checking to see if you *don't* have a profile on a social network. Yes, that could work against you too. They might wonder what you have to hide if you don't have one.

For most young people the transparency that social networks provide is refreshing. Right or wrong, you have to consider the bias of the people who might be hiring you. They might be older than you and trend towards being slightly less transparent, so monitor your social networks accordingly. You might think it's cool to have pictures of you and your friends toasting with beers in your hands at a party celebrating a winning college bowl game but...oops...three of the people in the picture look underage and you are now associated with that situation. Or, you might look drunk even if you weren't. Presumption of guilt by association isn't fair, but it is often a fact of life and an "unmentioned" reason why you might not get a job. Don't set yourself up for failure.

Always check your privacy settings to make sure that what you want seen is all that actually is being seen. Fortunately you can de-tag any questionable pictures your friends post and that you don't think are appropriate. There's nothing wrong with having fun, just display it in the context of the reputation and image you are trying to create for yourself. Think about it.

Chapter 8

~

15 key offer-letter negotiation points

If you ask for something you might get it.
It won't magically appear if you don't.

How do you know if that offer-letter you just got is a good deal or not? It seems like a good job where you can add a lot of value and has a fair compensation plan attached to it. But is it really a good offer? Should you take it?

Take a look at the salary and compare it to the area that you will be or are living in. Can you afford this job given all your financial obligations? Do you have a budget? Do you know what the cost of living is in the town that you would be living in? For more information type: *"cost of living comparison"* into your favorite search engine.

Run a net pay scenario so you can see what kind of bite federal, state and local taxes, Social Security, Medicare and state disability insurance take out of your paycheck.

For more information type: *"salary paycheck calculator"* into your favorite search engine. (More of this will be covered ahead, with examples, in Section III of the book.)

A good mentor will help guide you through the "Should I take this job?" thought process. There will be many components to your offer that you might not have thought about. There's always the base salary and for some people there can be commissions, a bonus or a profit sharing number. Is the bonus obtainable for you as a first year employee? And, what about other things in the offer that you'll need to consider?

While many HR people will tell you that the "employment package is the standard package" I haven't met a good HR person who can't get a little creative to sweeten the deal to get you hired. Are you getting married? Maybe you should negotiate some additional unpaid time off. Is the company a hot high-tech company? Maybe you can get a few more stock options. Is your job unique? Maybe they can get you a signing bonus of some kind or more stock options.

Don't wear out your welcome by over-negotiating before you've even started, but sometimes asking for more across many components of the offer can get you some additional perks. Ask your HR contact honestly if there are places where they can increase the offer. This works especially well if you already have an offer on the table from another company.

A NEGOTIATING TIP: As one recent graduate points out: "There is a fine line when it comes to negotiating. You don't want to come across as selfish or greedy. You want to be able to show your employer that you are worth more to the company than what you've just negotiated, but you don't want to come across as only having high expectations for your compensation."

If you are going to ask for more during the hiring process, make sure that you personally commit to giving more once you get the job.

If you are being hired for a position that will use your negotiation skills and you don't try to negotiate your employment package, it might be portrayed that you aren't hungry or strong enough.

When in doubt about how much more you could get to "close the deal" do some comparison-shopping with online recruiters or friends at other companies to see if your offer is at or above market. It's amazing what you can find on the web if you dig deeply enough.

It goes without saying, do not let your parents attempt to negotiate with or for you. They are not your agents and you need to stand on your own two feet. Your parents' advice is one thing – but getting involved directly in the hiring process is another. I'm not sure why I even have to say this...but it's happening more and more these days. One recent graduate, who is now employed by a Fortune 500 company, told me: "Millennials are very parent-dependent. Many of my friends, even the very smart and ambitious ones, have over-involved their parents in this process." Seriously? I couldn't wait to do things on my own and prove myself when I was getting started.

Here are 15 key offer letter negotiation points that you'll want to make sure you've covered (if applicable to your particular position):

1. **Base salary** – What is the base salary and how often is it paid out? Do I qualify for overtime?

2. **Bonus** – Is there a plan and is it tied to individual, department or company performance?

3. **Signing bonus** – If I'm in a high demand specialty do I get one? Do I have to pay it back if I leave the company in a certain time period or if I get laid-off? (Note: As with any other form of compensation signing bonuses are taxed like regular income.)

4. **Profit sharing or Stock Purchase Plans** – Are these plans offered and how do they work?

5. **Work related expenses** – Do I pay them and get reimbursed? Do I get mileage or a car allowance?

6. **Relocation costs** – If there is relocation what are the parameters? Hotel? Rental car? Moving expense limit? Timing?

7. **Health care benefits** – What does the employee pay out of their paycheck and what are the co-pays, co-insurance and deductibles? When does it go into effect?

8. **Stock options** – Are they available at my level and how do they vest?

9. **401K retirement plan** – Is there one and is there a company contribution? How much can I put in?

10. **Sick days / Well days** – How many per quarter? Is there a maximum on rolling them over? Do I get paid for them if I ever leave the company? Is there an annual cap where I will lose sick days after it's met?

11. Vacation time-off – How many weeks for a new employee? What's the approval process?

12. Unpaid time-off – Can I negotiate this if I get married or have a child and need extra time?

13. Maternity benefits – What are they? If my spouse has a baby do I get maternity time-off?

14. Salary reviews – How often are they and what's the process?

15. Advancement opportunities and requirements – When do I get to throw my "hat in the ring" for future job consideration? What is the promotion path for stellar performers? What kind of training is offered?

Many of these items may be outlined in your employment package, but not always. Make sure that you are satisfied with all the answers to your questions and that you are getting a fair deal. Once you sign the offer letter your negotiation comes to an end and you'll need to get down to work. Make sure that you are absolutely happy, as you don't want to be constantly haunted by the fact that the job wasn't what you thought it was or that you didn't get all you deserved.

Once you are "in" apply the same amount of energy
to your new job as you did to finding
and negotiating it and you'll be a success.

~~~

SECTION II:
Getting the most out of your first job

Chapter 9

~

Your "starter" job

If you've got a job (or are about to get one), that's great.

Congratulations.

Interestingly, college degrees no longer guarantee you a job. They probably never "really" did. It was just always assumed.

According to CNNMoney.com the "unemployment" rate for students used to hover just under 6%. These days it's just under 9%. If you do have a job, consider it an opportunity to learn more, and realize what you might not know. We never stop learning. If you don't have a job lined up yet, get started as soon as possible. Most of you probably feel like you should have started sooner than you did. Right?

Once you get your first job you might want to consider it a "starter" job. That may sound strange, but it really isn't. It's just realistic. Why? It's not the last job you will ever have. Your first job should be a *quid pro quo* or "even exchange" with your employer. You bring all your new knowledge, relentless enthusiasm and high energy to the table and your employer brings the offer of practical experience, and in some cases training. As long as everyone gets what he or she needs it all works.

At some point in your starter job there will be an imbalance. You'll be adding more or less value to the company than expected. If you are adding more value the chances are good you will be acknowledged, promoted, etc. If you are adding less value someone will find a way to let you know. That might mean getting fired, downsized, moved to a lesser job, etc. There are many names for it and when it happens it isn't necessarily your fault. Most people stay in their first job for 1-2 years, unless they get promoted. As far as building your resume, 1-2 years is a good time frame that shows stability.

The challenge is staying one step ahead of having someone else make your career decisions for you. This requires a keen sense of awareness of how you are doing in your job and getting feedback along the way...good or bad. Some people will never ask for feedback until annual review time – or if they get fired – and they might be shocked at the response when they felt they were doing a great job. Seek feedback whenever it's appropriate; just avoid coming across as being needy and in search of constant reinforcement. The trick to getting feedback is to *ask* for it. Employers, mentors, peers and even your college professors love to give feedback. All you have to do is ask for it.

You'll probably know when it's time to move on. You might be ready to take the next step in your career, or you might decide that what you are doing is "not for you." The worst case scenario is that someone might decide that for you. It's always better to be in control of the decision to do what's best for you.

If things don't work out in your first job that doesn't necessarily make you a bad employee. If you do leave a company, not by your own choice, try to figure out what you've learned from the experience and grow from it. It just might not have been a "good fit" and you will have an opportunity to try again at another company. No one is perfect. If there is something you could have done better make sure that becomes part of your game plan the next time around.

Chapter 10

~

10 ways to get the most out of your first job

Most people get a job, go to work, and then let life's little distractions consume them. They lose their "long-term view" of their job and life and get caught up in the gossip, petty behavior and all the other time-wasting traps that can consume their business day. They lose focus. They waste their energy and stop adding value to the world. At that point they become true 9-to-5'ers...not careerists. They do no more than what's expected of them. That might not be considered a bad gig for some, but it's not a great one either. That sounds boring to me. You always need to keep learning and growing. That means you need to stay on the tops of the waves in your job and not let them crash over you. I'd rather surf than drown any day. How about you?

What's the difference between those with successful careers and those who just get by? Here are some real world observations on how you can become successful early on in your career:

1. **Make your job a personally enjoyable experience.** Wake up and enjoy each day because you are learning and new doors can be opened for you. Not every moment of every day will be fun...but figure out a way to deal with it. Consider every task a short-term project that will teach you something. You won't be doing this forever. Ask yourself often: "What am I learning here?"

2. **Understand how your job fits in with the company.** Try to determine the value your job adds, and how it relates to other parts of the company. Over time you can use that information to get a sense of where your talents can be best used in the company and then head in that direction. Everything that you are learning is good for your cumulative knowledge. The more you learn the more valuable your skills will be across the company. Learning also allows you to find out what you may or may not want to do for the rest of your life.

3. **Think globally from within your department.** Don't get bogged down in the non-important petty minutia of the department you are working in. You don't have the time for it. Learn the details as quickly as you can but always have your eye on the bigger picture.

4. **Master every aspect of the job you were hired to do.** Aim to get great at your job on a repetitive basis, and then ask for more related responsibilities. Doing something right once or twice is beginner's luck, doing it well over and over is the sign of being a true professional. You gain more credibility as a valuable asset in your company by being consistently great at what you do.

5. **Volunteer for new assignments and take on challenging tasks.** Earn respect and be noticed as a standout by your superiors by asking for more to do. This assumes that you are great at accomplishing what you've already been assigned. These new assignments might include volunteering for additional work, committees, task forces or charities that your company is involved in. This is a good place to be a visible overachiever.

Employers love getting more than what
they think they paid for from their new hires.

6. **Work harder than others and put more time in initially.** This helps you get more experience within the company and shorten your learning curve. Who needs sleep when you are young? (Kidding somewhat on that...you do need balance in your life.) Just be aware that some people might resent you for your drive and for trying to make something of yourself. They might throw up roadblocks, so you'll need to work hard to not burn any bridges. It doesn't seem fair, but that's how some people are. It would be easy to make them an enemy... but that won't help you get where you are going.

A good rule to live by is that in the early stages of your career you should be willing to show up early or stay late. Be the one turning on, or shutting off, the lights. Your boss will take notice that he or she is leaving while you are still working hard, past the required hours. This strategy is especially effective if the quality and quantity of your work is exceptional. Where it doesn't work is when it takes you 10-12 hours to do 8 hours worth of work.

One recent graduate offers this perspective: "You should work for 'you,' keep your goals in mind and enjoy the challenge."

7. **Avoid the "us vs. them" mentality between other departments.** This is prevalent between departments in companies of all sizes. It's a huge waste of time...but you hear things like this a lot:

> "Those bean counters in accounting are killing me!"
> "The salespeople always overpromise."
> "The engineers think they know how to run this company."
> "Corporate never gets it right."

"All the marketing people can do is make pretty
brochures – they don't want to be accountable."
"The product development people are taking their
time."
"The _____ department thinks they are
"a gift" to the company."
And mostly any scenario in which:
Dept. A thinks Dept. B are a bunch of screw-ups.
And Dept. B thinks the same about Dept. A!

I've heard all of the above at some point in my career. All I can say is to try to understand why people in one department might have a negative opinion of people in other departments. It's usually because people can't take responsibility for their own actions so it makes them feel better to take others to task, rather than clean up their own act. It's an eye opener when people look from the outside in. The idea that everyone is in this together is a much better approach, but it takes cooperation and patience to pull it off. It also assumes that everyone is mostly competent throughout the organization. You'll find out soon enough if that assumption about competence is true.

INTERESTING OBSERVATIONS: One recent graduate who went to work in a large corporate environment offers this perspective: "Try to think of each department as a customer and treat them with that respect. You need them, so appreciate them for what they bring to the company that you are also a part of."

Another issue that could pop-up is when inter-departmental battles make their way into e-mail and on social networking sites in the form of gossip, slander, whining and complaining. That same student above says: "Every e-mail should be written with the understanding and mentality that your CEO or a judge could one day read it." Those are great words to live by.

8. **Network with others inside and outside the company.** Have a higher-level view of what's going on in your company and the marketplace. Take some time to look at your company from the outside in. Keep reading analyst reports and business news. Never disclose any insider information, even with people you work with, especially when you are out in public. Treat everything you are told as though it's confidential.

9. **Be genuinely curious about the business.** Be knowledgeable about your company and the competition. Keep your eyes open for the next great business opportunity and potential partnerships, but don't overstep your boundaries. Think "big picture"... like you might run the company some day, but keep that idea to yourself so that your co-workers or superiors won't think that you are angling for their job.

10. **Have great mentors.** Always have a trusted sounding board inside and outside of your company. The more people you have helping you succeed the faster it will happen, and the sooner you can start giving back by also being a mentor.

Chapter 11

~

10 personal attributes of successful new employees

Competitive drive will differentiate you and create success. The more you have of it the more you'll get out of life.

Ever wonder why some employees are successful in their careers and others are not? It often has a lot to do with how they approach their first job. Successful people view their job as a privilege and an opportunity. They apply what they have learned in college, but their eyes remain wide open to learning new things.

Here are 10 attributes that can help you be more successful:

1. **Take personal responsibility for your actions.** One of the biggest problems in the working world, and life in general, is lack of personal responsibility. You see it at the CEO level and down through the organizational chart. You see it in friends and family. If you dig deep you will also see it in yourself. Everyone can find someone or something else to blame for the poor decisions they have made. If you are doing this, STOP IT!

   I have found that the moment you can accept responsibility for your actions in the presence of others you will begin to grow. Just because others won't take personal responsibility for their actions doesn't mean that you shouldn't. Making a mistake and admitting to it is extremely liberating, and not in the "you just got fired for it" kind of way!

   Don't get caught blaming someone or something for a mistake you made. Take the ethical high road and you'll always be on the right track. Just don't look to most of corporate America for your role models. They are few and far between. A recent graduate backs me up with this thought: "Always show maturity and professionalism, then fix your mistake and be sure not to repeat it." Another recent graduate told me: "Self-awareness is the first step to success in leadership – be aware of your weaknesses in order to find a good balance with the strengths of others."

2. **Have good listening skills.** We all seem to graduate with the feeling that we are on top of the world. You

should enjoy every minute of it. Once you get into the real world you realize that you don't know as much as you think you do. That's OK.

This is a great time to apply your listening skills while you see what is going on around you. Observe how your manager and their manager work with each other, conduct meetings, deal with clients, work with the exec team, etc. There's book smart and street smart. You want to be both, but the latter takes actual experience. To get there you'll need to learn to listen and observe.

As eager as we are to share our ideas we sometimes need to be careful about interrupting others (unconsciously, or otherwise). At this stage of your career hear what others have to say and do more listening than talking.

Your ability to learn new things is directly related to your listening skills. If you are really hearing what someone is saying then you can get into asking clarifying questions along the way. The more questions you ask the more you learn. Just don't over do it. You'll know when you are getting close to "the answer" because the questions will become very specific.

The opposite end of the spectrum is starting the conversation by asking questions that are too broad or too vague. You don't want it to appear that you have done no research on the basics in preparation for the discussion. If you do your homework in advance and have specific questions you can always add to them as you go along. No matter how many questions you ask, good listening (as well as understanding the answers) is always your first priority.

3. **Be genuine.** If you are a genuine person you'll go far. If you spend a lot of time trying to act how you think others would want you to act there's a good chance you'll go

down in flames. Going with the flow and applying the listening rule from above is one thing, being two-faced in your company is another. Acting fake won't get you very far. I've seen plenty of people crash-and-burn on this.

4. **Be open and honest.** If you think something is being done wrong try to understand why...and then, if you think it's still wrong, find an appropriate way to express it. It's refreshing when people can say what they think, as long as it's intelligent. If you think something is being done illegally or unethically then find a way to say so... but only after you are convinced and have proof. Just spouting off with an uninformed opinion, or hearsay from others, will always get you in trouble.

   One recent graduate had an interesting thought on this: "Understand that not everyone will agree with every decision made in your company. Be open to feedback and debates...and address them appropriately." At the end of the day it's not a matter of who is right, but what is right for the company.

5. **Have a positive attitude.** Don't enter the building without it. No one likes working with someone who is negative and whiney. I think the correct term is "doggie downer" – and I'm not talking about a yoga pose. People who are moving up in an organization tend to distance themselves from whiney people. If you are going to be working 10-12 hour days wouldn't you rather be around people who are upbeat and fun to be around? You need to be the same, and lead that charge. It's called leadership.

6. **Show personal integrity.** Integrity is all you take from one job to the next. People appreciate integrity because it builds trust. If you've done something wrong, and not owed up to it, the word will get out. Some of the

most successful people I know are the ones that have stayed in an industry and grown with it. They couldn't have gotten where they are with a lack of integrity. Yes, they've made honest mistakes and they've fixed them, and then continued to move forward.

7. **Dress appropriately.** Dress codes are different by company and even by department. Being at the top-end of the middle range of the wardrobe spectrum in your department shows some class and maybe a nod towards that next-level job you will someday qualify for. Over-dressing shows a touch of "I'm better than you," while under-dressing makes you look like a slob. Know the differences and play the upper-middle ground until you see what's appropriate and comfortable in the group you work with.

When I was getting ready to go to college I got a good piece of advice from a best friend. She said: "Take enough clothes to school to get by for a few weeks. See what everyone else is wearing and then make your choices according to what works for you." The same applies in business.

BE A FASHION VICTIM AT YOUR OWN RISK: If you show up to most jobs, at least the corporate ones, with your pants around your butt and your underwear showing you won't be scoring any points with anyone... no matter how cool it looked in college. Even if it's some nice looking underwear! Every generation has their "fashion statements" that annoy prior generations. In my generation it was bell-bottom jeans that caused the drama with adults. Go figure.

8. **Be resourceful and self-sufficient.** Figure out ways to solve problems, who to ask for help, when to involve others and when to do things yourself. It's called being resourceful and self-sufficient. This is also known as

45

being a self-starter. Managers appreciate this mentality. And almost everyone else appreciates this too. Know when to take a personal initiative or when to build group consensus. It takes some time to figure out what works best, so be open to making mistakes, offering apologies and, learning and doing better the next time around.

9. **Live a balanced life and stay in shape.** If you work all the time and succumb to the vending machine regularly you will gain more than the 20 pounds you did as a freshman in college. Remember that? It sucked didn't it? Take "walking" meetings when possible and avoid rewards that are eating or drinking based. Make it about something else. Enjoy balancing your personal life and your work life. If you can combine them to your satisfaction and make healthy choices you will be on the right path.

10. **Have fun!** This might be the most important tip of all. There is no reason to work and not have fun. Work is a four-letter word to some, but so is the word *love*. If you *love* your work it will get you a lot farther than if you *hate* it. If you *love* your work it won't even seem like work. Enjoy what you do and the experiences you are getting. Your first job only happens once and those experiences can't be replicated. Make the most of it and you will have excellent lessons for the future.

Chapter 12

~

5 tips for finding meaningful mentors

Mentors are a significant component to a successful career. They can help you in many respects, and not all of it is work related. Find ones who are important to you personally and to your career. Mentoring is becoming more and more of the "in" thing these days. The insight of those who have gone before you is invaluable in helping to point you in the right direction.

1. **Make it a goal to find one, a great one.** Look for at least one person you trust to be a mentor and who has no vested interested in you other than your personal success. They can come from anywhere, just make sure they are great at what they do and will tell it like it is. The best place to find them can be at industry events, on business networking sites, through your friends in the business, by joining trade associations, and attending lectures and fundraisers, etc. Once you've found a potential mentor go to your favorite search engine and social networking sites to learn more about them. You'd be amazed at what you can find. You might have a connection that you didn't know about.

   If you are having trouble finding a "real world" mentor you can always use your college professors as a fallback. They already know you and can help guide you in the early going.

2. **Keeping in touch.** If you've made initial contact with someone you'd like to be your mentor, ask if it's OK to

keep in touch with him or her to share ideas from time-to-time and seek their advice. Take a casual approach. Don't be surprised if you hear "no" sometimes when asking someone to be your mentor. Don't take it personally since they are busy people.

When you do meet try to make it face-to-face. These meetings are more memorable and personal. Quick e-mails are fine once a relationship is established, but they shouldn't replace real meetings.

3. **Make it a two-way street.** Don't just contact your mentor when you need something. Send them newsworthy items or a "heads-up" on unique or obscure industry events that you think they might be interested in from time-to-time (and that they probably would not know about). That will help build the relationship and keep it flourishing.

4. **Ask to be challenged.** Use your mentor to help challenge what you think and explore new thoughts and opportunities. Ask them for ideas on how to approach solving a problem or how you could do something better.

5. **Return the favor.** Be a mentor to others when the time is right. You can be an effective mentor at almost any time because there will always be those younger or more inexperienced than you who can use great advice from someone who has been there. Only go down this path if you feel like you can add honest value to someone else's life.

What about finding a mentor inside your company?

Proceed with caution here. Why? Your first inclination might be to have someone you work for, or someone that is in your department, be your mentor. I would recommend against that. Your boss or others close-by might have a certain agenda that isn't always in your best career interest. It's better to find someone who you respect but is removed from your day-to-day efforts.

Be politically astute when picking a good mentor. Look for someone whom you can trust, who could act as a role model for you, and who has good visibility inside the company.

Chapter 13

~

20 tips for meetings with "higher-ups" in the company

There will always be someone above you in the hierarchy of a company. Even if you are ultimately the CEO there's always the Board of Directors there to give you guidance.

If you have a mentor who is above you (and who isn't at this point?) in the company then you get to learn what it's like to deal with those higher-ups. If your mentor isn't that elevated (and that's OK) then you might be casually exposed to the higher-ups through your association with them.

Dealing with those above you is actually a lot easier than it seems. Just treat them like a regular person. This works because people are sucking-up to them all day, they are constantly being asked to make decisions, or their boss is meeting with them and assigning tasks. If you treat them like a regular person they will most likely treat you the same. That level of familiarity will help get you get to their peer level faster.

There are five reasons (and probably more) why you would be meeting with a higher-up at this point in your career:

1) To meet them so they know who you are
2) To possibly have them be a mentor
3) To be promoted or demoted
4) To update them on a project you are working on,
   or be assigned a new one
5) To be commended or disciplined for something

Try to determine which one it is before you get in the door. If they ask you for the meeting just ask for some clarification on what the purpose of the meeting is so that you can be prepared. If they don't tell you then be ready for anything!

Here are 20 tips for meetings with higher-ups. How you use these tips will vary depending on which kind of meeting you are being invited to from the list above.

1. Remember that talking to a higher-up is, as always, just a conversation.
2. Show respect for the person *and* their position. If you can get their bio or LinkedIn profile information in advance of the meeting to learn more about them.
3. Have a sense of humor but never one that is "off-color" – you never know when the higher-up might be testing you or actually have issues.
4. Be genuine in your conversation, and open and honest in your responses.
5. Have a personal goal for the meeting. What do you want to accomplish?
6. Maintain a high level of professionalism.
7. The more time you spend with a higher-up the better you will get to know them – just don't rush the process. Getting to know someone takes time.
8. Try to understand their demeanor and make sure it is compatible with yours.
9. Be buttoned-down and organized, but relaxed, in your meeting approach.
10. Be prepared with great questions and don't be afraid to take notes.

11. Be succinct in your conversation.
12. If appropriate, ask them how they have handled certain work related issues or problems that have come up.
13. Also, ask them what mistakes they made on their way up and what their recommendations would be to you to keep from making the same mistakes.
14. Don't "dis" any of your peers or your boss.
15. Don't try to sell or boast about your accomplishments at the expense of others.
16. If you are being "taken to task" (i.e.: in trouble) for something, try to understand why and accept the criticism. If you have an opportunity to provide feedback then do so. Avoid pointing fingers at others if you share in part of the blame.
17. Do more listening than talking – you are there to learn from them.
18. Set realistic expectations if you are being asked to do something.
19. Close the meeting with next steps and a follow-up meeting.
20. Deliver on whatever you promised with accuracy and timeliness.

Chapter 14

~

Setting initial 30/60/90 day goals

While you are getting acclimated to you new job you might want to work with your boss to set some short-term measurable goals. That way you can start getting a sense of accomplishment and know how you are doing. A good place to start is with 30/60/90 day work goals, but have a willingness to adjust the time frame in which they need to be accomplished, depending on what they are.

Make sure your short-term goals are agreeable to you and attainable - even if you have to stretch a bit. These goals should be specific to the job you were hired to do and might include: doing your weekly reports by a specified time or day each week, calling a certain number of clients, learning a new task, meeting with a certain number of people or internal partners inside the company, etc. Come up with five or so that are measurable and attainable, with some effort, over a reasonable time period. That way you'll know that you are accomplishing something real.

You can also set personal 30/60/90 day goals that only you know about. They might be to exceed the goals that your boss gave you or an entirely different set of goals. Your personal goals might be: to take a walk or have lunch with everyone in your department each month, or to meet casually with your peers in other departments to build longer-term relationships. The choice is yours, just make sure they are meaningful and add value to your career.

Make sure that you write these goals down so you can hold yourself accountable. Just trying to remember them won't work. You will get a feeling of achievement as you check-off these goals and continue to move up the learning curve.

Chapter 15

~

Getting better-connected in business

It's whom you know, what you know, and how you use it.

Facebook was great in high school and college. It's still great for keeping up with your friends, but I doubt you'd want the professionals you work with to see what you've got posted on your Wall. Right? Now it's time to get better connected for business.

If you've used LinkedIn to set up your resume, you already have an account and you can start adding business connections to it. If you haven't already, set up a LinkedIn page at linkedin.com.

You can start creating your business network immediately. Use all the tools LinkedIn has to offer. Do updates every once in a while, but don't give the impression that you are constantly hanging-out online. Never disclose any insider data or post any complaints about your company on any of your social networks.

Do more than just sign-up and collect business friends; interact with them when appropriate - and not just when you need something. Ask the people you trust if they will mentor you in some way. (You've heard much of this previously in the book.) Sure, there will be overlap between your Facebook and LinkedIn friends but these social networks serve two different purposes. I have selected just two social networks to associate with: Facebook and LinkedIn. I just don't have the time in my day for maintaining any more than that.

You can also take the same approaches outlined when you are networking for a job. Consider getting involved in national and local industry organizations and networking events. They are occurring constantly if you know where to look for them. The business section of your local newspaper or your town's local business journal, if it has one, will have listings. Also, check the calendars in the appropriate trade media. When you go to an event take plenty of your business cards with you. Make meaningful new friendships, especially if there is a possibility that you will both be able to add value to each other's careers. This can also be helpful in finding a great mentor.

> EXCHANGING BUSINESS CARDS: In addition to giving your card out, make sure you get the other person's card. While this seems obvious it is a common newbie mistake. If they don't have a business card, never assume that when you ask the other person to e-mail you that they actually will. Most people will forget. If they don't have their business card, tap their info into your mobile device or write it down before you go your separate ways, then follow-up with them at a later time - usually 24-48 hours, while they are still fresh in your memory. See if they are on LinkedIn and connect with them. Always remind someone who you are and how you met when you try to reconnect with them.
>
> What if they don't have a business card? Pull out one of your cards and have them write their contact information on it. Make sure that includes the correct spelling of their name, and a legible phone number and e-mail address.

Chapter 16

~

15 group-meeting etiquette tips

The first couple of group meetings that you attend in a new company can provide some drama if you aren't prepared. Here are some ideas on proper meeting etiquette.

There are advantages to group meetings: They are a meeting point for getting focused on company or departmental issues and they give you status updates on other areas in the company that you might be interacting with.

There are also problems with group meetings: They start late, they run long, they waste a ton of time, and they take you away from doing your actual job. If you are in meetings all day you will be working all night. Unfortunately, real work rarely gets done in meetings...it just gets critiqued or assigned.

Here are tips on how to handle group meetings:

1. **Be "right on time."** If you are invited to a meeting, get there a few minutes before it starts. Maybe a little earlier if you don't know everyone in the room. If it's appropriate, introduce yourself to people who you don't know. Don't appear over anxious by showing up 5-15 minutes early. People will think you don't have enough work to do. Chances are, with a "right on time" meeting strategy, you'll probably be the first one there anyway. It pays to ask around and see what the company culture is on the timeliness of showing up to meetings.

MORE THOUGHTS ABOUT BEING "RIGHT-ON-TIME":
- Show respect for the person who is running the meeting. It seems easy until you're the one who has to do it for your first time.
- When you show up "right-on-time" be ready to get to work immediately. Don't sit down and then get up and go get coffee or engage in mindless chit-chat or other time wasters.
- The notion of "showing up 15 minutes early" is bogus to me. It's one of those *often-repeated myths* about meetings. If you are in a service industry and your time is billable, or you are paid for performance, you are wasting 15 minutes of usable/profitable time.
- If your boss tells you to "show up 15 minutes early or you're late" he or she doesn't have much faith that you will be showing up on time. Think about why that is being said to you.
- *And most importantly:* Don't be the *last* one in the room who holds up the start of the meeting. That's worse than showing up too early.

2. **If it's not your meeting, don't try to control it.** If it's not your meeting just learn and respond when appropriate. It's better to analyze the situation before jumping in. That's a classic newbie mistake. You also have a chance to watch how others handle running a meeting. It's a lot harder than you think.

3. **What are the goals, agenda and time limit?** If appropriate, ask for the goal and agenda for the meeting, in advance. If it's a pre-existing agenda keep it in your folder so you know what to expect. Meetings can get out of control quickly without an agenda...and little gets accomplished. I got to a point in my career where I refused to go to meetings unless I saw an agenda/goal in advance so that I knew the meeting would be a good use of my time. I'm not sure that you get that option if you are just out of college.

4. **Be organized.** Have a folder for the meeting (digital or paper). Keep everything associated with the meeting in one place. I put a date on the meeting folder and always include a "my follow-up" section.

5. **Come prepared.** If you are presenting in the meeting be ready for it and be succinct. You don't get paid by the word, you get paid to get things done.

6. **Take notes.** It's easy to think that you will remember everything that went on in the meeting, who said what, and any responsibilities that you might have. I'm not sure that you'll be thinking that after your third meeting of the day and tenth meeting of the week. Write things down.

7. **Follow-up.** If you have been given follow-up tasks make sure that you do so in a timely matter. Make it a personal goal to follow-up in a specific time frame.

8. **Getting out first.** If you are in a meeting where each team member is reporting weekly status, try to go first. If you don't need to hear what the other team members are reporting ask, before the meeting, if you can be excused after you give your update. If you need to hear how other members of the team are interacting then be there and use that time wisely.

9. **Avoid distractions.** If you are reviewing e-mail, sending text messages, or checking Facebook (unless you work there!) while others are reporting, and you are supposed to be paying attention, you might as well not even be at the meeting. I make it a point to ask anyone that I saw who I feel is distracted in a meeting what they thought of the last comment that was made. That usually gets people focused...no one wants to be called out next or look stupid.

10. If you are called on to run a meeting, apply what you read above and:

- Don't be over-bearing or over-anxious.
- Ask for help from others if you need it.
- Have a meeting goal and agenda
- Set a time-limit on the meeting – in 30 or 60 minute segments
- Send out the goal/agenda well in advance – which does not mean 5 minutes before the meeting starts
- Be more organized
- Cover follow-up from the last meeting at the beginning of the next meeting or when appropriate throughout the meeting
- Don't waste time, keep the meeting moving along
- Be succinct
- Make the meeting meaningful and enjoyable
- Respect the opinion of others
- Keep people focused on topics related to the meeting
- Appreciate the time of those who are attending
- Assign follow-up tasks (if you have the power to)
- Keep track of the follow-up assignments
- In between meeting dates make sure that people are on track to accomplish their follow-up tasks
- Finish within the time limit and thank everyone for contributing and helping the meeting finish on time
- Always strive to meet your meeting goals. If you can't meet your meeting goals add them to the next meeting's agenda - and remember to cover them as "old business" at the next meeting

Chapter 17

~

10 tips for promoting your ideas inside your company

Ideas are nothing, until someone makes them happen.

Once you get settled in your job and figure out where the light switches and bathrooms are, you will start noticing all kinds of opportunities for improvement inside your company. It's the "curse" of being the bright new person with an education.

Let's say you come-up with a brilliant idea that you think your company could benefit from. You did a great job selling "you" to the company when you first got your job, but from this point on you will need to change gears from selling yourself to promoting your ideas.

While they may be *your* ideas they are really ideas that are in the best interest of the company. And that's the way you'll want to present them. No one wants to hear: "I have a brilliant idea, I think we should do _____." It's too self-serving because it focuses on the word "I." A better approach might be this: "There's an idea I've been casually kicking around with others inside the company and it might be in our best interest to consider it, it goes like this: _____." See the difference?

For the rest of your career you will need to promote your ideas in presentations, executive briefings, and while working with others to accomplish day-to-day tasks and long-term projects. Whatever idea you are promoting, if it's *all* about you it will *only* be about you. People probably won't respond well to that kind of self-promotion.

Also, if there's an opportunity to be promoted in the future you will need to promote how your ideas and accomplishments have helped the company, not all the typical: "I'm great and I did this, then I did that...and it was all my idea" kind of stuff. Your superiors probably already know why you are the right person for your next job because of the team effort you've shown and the leadership roles you've taken. No need for a "hard sell" here. I'm not saying that you shouldn't take credit for your ideas, but there are ways that don't put the spotlight on you and make it the "YOU Show." I'm suggesting a softer approach.

Learning to promote your ideas isn't easy. I'm going to assume here that you are, or will be, part of a team. Here are 10 tips that might help you get your ideas across more effectively:

1. **Introducing a new idea.** Ask your boss how new ideas are brought into the department or company. If you get the impression that your boss is an idea killer, and not a new idea supporter, you might want to suggest some lesser ideas first to "take a temperature" on how far your idea might get and what the process is. If your boss is an idea killer then try to find some other avenue to get ideas in play – but not the ideas your boss has already said no to (the lesser ideas).

2. **It's just a conversation.** Remember that when you are promoting ideas you are only having a conversation with others. It's not a sell job. This is important when you are trying to get your points across to find a way to help solve a problem. (This should sound familiar by now.)

3. **Getting the discussion rolling.** Sometimes having the initial idea and getting the discussion rolling is what gets the idea heading in the right direction. If you get involved in the conversation by saying "Have we thought about _____? Anyone have some ideas?" See what the rest of the group comes up with.

They might just "finish the sentence" that you started with your initial idea.

4. **Inserting ideas.** Another approach might be that once the conversation is started you can insert parts of your ideas along the way, as suggestions. See if you can get buy-in for those ideas, one piece at a time.

5. **Create group ideas.** Being the leader of the group that comes up with a great idea is often more powerful than coming up with the idea yourself. You can always benefit from the input of others (good and bad) in the brain-storming process.

6. **Rapport & fun.** Build rapport within your team when you are brainstorming new ideas. Make the meetings fun. Keep it upbeat and creative. Allow people to open-up and share their ideas. If you have a controlling or overbearing personality this will be difficult. Avoid "hi-jacking" the process.

7. **Test-drive your ideas.** Try your ideas on a few people whose opinion you trust before everyone gets in the room. Be prepared to make changes to your ideas once you get feedback from others.

8. **Make it everyone's idea.** Once you do get feedback from others "your idea" becomes "everyone's idea" and should be presented that way. No one likes to have their ideas stolen, especially without being given credit for their thoughts, so give credit when it is due.

9. **Simplifying ideas.** New ideas can be confusing to others because most people don't like change. Simplifying complicated ideas will help others understand them better. As one recent graduate points out: "This means putting things in terms that others will understand, not the terms that you are used to. Never assume others

know what you know. They will just agree with you so they don't have to admit they don't know something. That eliminates the opportunity for them to learn something and get agreement and buy-in of a new idea."

10. **Make the team the hero.** At the end of the meeting it may be apparent that there are better ideas than just yours. Make the team the "hero" when it comes to coming up with ideas. The important part is that a good idea comes to life. If you are the person behind enough good ideas that can be executed on, it will be pretty obvious to those above you.

~~~

SECTION III:
Money & Your first paycheck

Chapter 18
~
What to do with graduation gifts

Take the cash and put it away.
Then make it last as long as you can.

If you have the option of cash when it comes to graduation gifts, take it! Tell your relatives that you prefer cash, no matter what the amount, because you are going to save it and start off your life the right way. They'll be impressed, and perhaps even pleasantly surprised!

Put the money in a savings account and use it as a cushion while you are transitioning between college and your first job. Resist the temptation to go blow all this money like everyone else around you will be doing. Once it's gone, it's gone. I've always viewed gifts as "bonuses" and tried to use them as a way to put me in a better place in life. That better place shouldn't include a $300 pair of designer shoes.

If you must spend your money on something, take 10% of your gift money and buy something that's a nice memory of what you've just accomplished. Make sure it passes the test of enduring over time, and that includes experiences and memories.

REAL LIFE EXAMPLE: Many people buy a high school class ring...and typically wear it until they go to college (about a year). Then that couple of hundred bucks that was spent on the class ring sits in a drawer forever... because high school was so yesterday and you want to be associated with the future since you're in now college. I fell for it and a lot of others did too. Take the cash instead...and save it.

The lesson here is that all the things you think you need at the moment because you are caught up in whatever hysteria is being promoted to you, well...you probably don't really need them at all.

When I guest lecture at universities I ask students: "Do any of you want a new car for graduation?" Hands immediately are raised up with lots of smiles on everyone's faces. Then I ask: "What would a new car that you'd want to be seen driving cost today...maybe $20,000?" They nod yes.

Then the conversation continues like this:

"Here's something you might not be expecting to hear: If your parents offer you a new car say 'thank you' and then politely ask for the same amount in cash. Yes, cash. Put $4,000 into a savings account and $4,000 into a starter Emergency Fund. An Emergency Fund is equal to 3-6 months of living expenses – it is different than a savings account because you *only* use it in case of a dire financial need. Take $10,000 and buy a 3-4 year old version of 'that' car you'd want be seen in. You might consider financing $2,000 of the car to start building your credit. If you do, pay it off after a year. Put $2,000 into a repair account. (NOTE: That's not a 'bling out my car' repair account.) If the car proves to be super reliable then you might want to move some of that repair money over to your savings account or Emergency Fund. You might also decide to pay off some student loans and then start building an investment/retirement/savings account."

Here's how it looks in spreadsheet format:

Savings Account	$4,000 (or $5,000)
Emergency Fund	$4,000 (or $5,000)
Nice Used Car	$10,000 (or $8,000 and finance $2,000)
Repair Account	<u>$2,000</u>
Total	$20,000

While the car will last only for a while, the ultimate return on your investments and peace of mind from having savings will last a lot longer.

Chapter 19

~

The truth about money

Money gives you more freedom.
It's only evil if you allow it to be.
It helps you get many things out of life.
But on it's own it won't set you free.

I majored in finance and economics in college. I love playing with numbers and financial scenarios. So I did a little calculating to give you an idea of just how much money might flow through your hands by the time you turn 65.

I'm going to keep this simple. First, let's say that you earn the average $48,000 first year salary for a college graduate at age 22. (According to The National Association of Colleges and Employers the 2010 average was $48,351.) Then let's say that your salary grows 5% every year including promotions, bonuses, merit increases, job changes, etc., and let's also assume that you save 10% of your gross salary "Off the Top" before any deductions.

Let's also assume that your savings become investments and grow 6% a year. This is highly conservative and what many investors consider to be the new reality for investment growth. Keep in mind that this is all before federal income and capital gains taxes, inflation and personal expenses, etc. It's much easier to visualize it this way because no one knows what all those other variables will be. This is why it makes sense to pay into your savings and investment accounts first.

OK, now you have all the basic assumptions. So, let's see what happens:

Before taxes you will have grossed over $7,254,864 during your working lifetime. Congratulations! If you save 10% of that gross amount each year and it grows 6% a year, at 65 you will have over $769,000 in your savings/investment account.

Congratulations...again.

The hard part will be actually doing it.

This analysis doesn't take into consideration any matching funds for a 401(k) that your company might provide, and it doesn't take into consideration any Social Security benefits as an additional source of income when you retire. It's never a good idea to count on Social Security, as it may not exist when you retire. It also doesn't take into consideration any profit sharing, stock purchase plans, or stock options that you might earn in an emerging market company you might work for or invest in.

All of those things are in addition to my basic calculations. So you could be in for a whole lot more. But it won't be automatic. You have be consciously focused on getting it all in motion. What keeps all this money in your personal accounts or puts it in someone else's hands are the financial decisions that you make. As you can see from the above, we are talking about a lot of money. For some people it will be a lot more, for others a lot less.

Money can be a great tool to help you get what you want out of life. Money seems so simple, but it's really quite complex. It can be put to good use, or not. It can help people, or not. The choices you make regarding it will determine that outcome. Choose wisely.

Chapter 20

~

Does money buy happiness?

Buying everything you want isn't what it's all about.
Enjoying what you have is what makes you truly happy.

You get your first job, and your friends get their first jobs. Some of your friends will make more money, and some will make less. Will making any additional money make you or them any happier? In some respects, yes...up to a point.

According to a report in the *Proceedings of the National Academy of Sciences*, happiness does get "better" as incomes rise...up to about $75,000 a year. After that point happiness didn't increase, but as income increased past that amount so did a sense of success and well-being.

Keep in mind that there is a big difference between income and wealth. *Income* is what you make, *wealth* is what you keep and grow. People can somehow manage to have high incomes but minimal or negative net worth. Yes, it's unbelievable but true. Go figure. You have to be "working" *(sarcasm added)* very hard to accomplish that.

Many (OK, most) of us are taught to be consumption junkies from a young age. Big screen TVs, bigger houses, new cars, computers and personal electronics are considered signs of success when you become an adult. But are they, really?

67

Do they give us more peace-of-mind or are they just more stuff to worry about?

If you achieve a $75,000 a year income or more, why not just bank and invest that additional money to extend your sense of success and well-being well into your future years? I took the approach of "banking" all my commission and bonus checks when I was younger. They came in handy later.

Need an example of how blowing your money isn't worth it? Some people like to reward themselves with big presents for major accomplishments. Let's suppose you decide to reward yourself with a new car. The excitement of that new car wears off well before the last payment is made. Personal experience tells me it's usually around payment number 12...with at least 36 more payments remaining! Meanwhile the sense of security of having money in the bank is priceless and long term.

The big question is: Does happiness equate more to a shiny new material possession, or a life experience that you will never forget, or celebrating a personal accomplishment, or putting a smile on someone else's face? It might be all depending on your point in life, but in a "bigger picture" sense, which is more important? And how much money do you need to accomplish any or all of them? At the end of it all, it's really not about the money; it's about the mentality towards it.

Now is a good time to calibrate your thinking about what it means to be successful and how you celebrate it. How do *you* define success? Think about it. Make a goal for yourself and then take the steps to achieve and celebrate it.

Chapter 21

~

Focus on your FICO score
...it's your new GPA

You needed a great GPA to get into college, and now you'll need a great FICO score to get the best credit. Your FICO score is probably more important now than your GPA ever was. FICO is an acronym for the Fair Isaac Corporation. Both Fair and Isaac are the names of the two engineers that founded the credit scoring company in 1956. (Source: Wikipedia)

According to myFICO.com your FICO score is based on a combination of all these variables:

> 35% Payment history
> 30% Amounts owed
> 15% Length of credit history
> 10% New credit
> 10% Types of credit used

Scores range from 300-850. The higher your score the better. With the economy being the way it has been, higher credit ratings have been needed to accomplish what lower ratings could have achieved just years ago.

There are a lot of opinions on what are the best credit score ranges. Here's my take (with data from Bloomberg):

> 350 – 500   NOT GONNA HAPPEN
> 500 – 579   WORSE - highest rates
> 580 – 619   BAD - probably "sub-prime" rates

620 – 659   OK - this is a "gray zone" depending
            on the type of lender
660 – 719   GOOD - minimum for those making
            major credit purchases
720 – 759   VERY GOOD - the tipping-point for
            getting the best rates
760 – 850   EXCELLENT

LESSON LEARNED: Get your FICO score up before making any major credit-based purchases.

You can get all three of your credit *reports* for free...really. But you can't get your credit *scores* truly for free.

According to creditcards.com: "The Fair and Accurate Credit Transactions Act (FACTA) provides that the three major credit reporting bureaus (Equifax, Experian, and TransUnion) must provide a free copy of your credit report every 12-month period. You can call 1-877-322-8228, visit annualcreditreport.com or complete the annual credit request form at www.ftc.gov/credit and mail it to: Annual Credit Report Request Service, P.O. Box 105281, Atlanta, GA 30348-5281."

Be aware that all three credit rating agencies would love to sell you their own brand of credit rating scores and additional ser-vices. You do not need to sign up for these services to get your free annual credit report.

As research for this chapter, I got my free credit report from each of the three reporting agencies using annualcreditreport.com. The process took about 5-10 minutes for each agency. You fill out some info online, get the report online and be able to print it out. It's pretty easy so there is no excuse for not doing it. Look at the reports while you are still online and see if there is any information that needs to be corrected. You can fill out an online form with each credit-reporting agency to open a "dispute" file and start the process of cleaning up your record.

What's in your credit report? It contains: your current and previous addresses, employment data/history, credit accounts with payment history, and any inquiries into your credit history from potential lenders or other credit-checking agencies.

What's not in your credit report is your FICO score. That is a separate number that is compiled based on the combination of variables listed above.

I looked at the credit report that I felt was the most accurate for me and then went back to myFICO.com and bought my specific "myFICO Standard" score from that agency. In my case it was the Equifax myFICO Standard score. It sounds a little complicated but you want to buy the myFICO score that is created by the most accurate credit reporting agency and not the credit reporting agency's own "home grown" version of your credit score. Not surprisingly, Equifax calls their version: The Equifax Credit Score™ and it's not the same as your myFICO score. Your real FICO score is what the lenders care about. It's worth the $19.95 (for one report). Once a year should do it.

After doing a lot of looking online you'll see that many sites do offer your credit *score* for free. But they aren't really free. There are always strings attached to these offers, namely that you have to sign up for an "offer" program, or a trial of a monthly credit monitoring service that requires you to give out your credit card info. If you do, be sure to remember to cancel the "free" offer before they start billing you for it. Many of these "free credit" offers are scams – so be careful.

With your free annual credit reports mandated by the government and your FICO score from myFICO.com, you will have all the info you need to keep an eye on, and improve, your credit.

Credit Tips:

1. **Shop around** – When you are applying for credit, whether it's for a house or a car (hopefully you are

paying mostly cash for that car) or some other type of consumer loan make sure you shop around and ask specifically if you are getting the best rate available for your credit score.

2. **Work it** – You have to work to keep your credit score high by paying your bills on time, and not maxing out your available credit. If you opened up a credit card when you were in college keep it open and make minimal charges to it that you pay off each month. That will set an early timeline for your credit and show a payment history. The length of time you've had credit helps with your score and if you cancel that card you cancel the timeline.

3. **Know the downsides** – Liz Pulliam Weston, a noted financial author and contributor to MSNMoney.com, asked FICO to show how using credit poorly can affect your credit score. The two measures that will be most important to you right now are: What happens when you max out a credit card; and what happens if you have a 30 day late payment? It will definitely hurt your credit.

	680 FICO score
Maxed Out Credit Card	-10 to -30 points
30 Day Late Payment	-60 to -80 points

	780 FICO score
Maxed Out Credit Card	-25 to -45 points
30 Day Late Payment	-90 to -110 points
(Source: FICO)	

Those two categories above add up to 65% of your credit rating. If you mess up on these it will cost you a lot more when you go to get a car loan, home loan, etc.

For the most current tips on improving your credit scores type: "*improve my credit scores*" in your favorite search engine. And again: Always be on the lookout for scammers.

Chapter 22

~

What is *your* #1 financial goal after you graduate and get your first job?

Want to make your dreams come true?
First, you need to have a goal.
Second, you need to set a deadline for it.
Third, you need to do it.

Deciding what your financial goals are isn't easy. What exactly is a "goal" anyway? The important rule about setting a goal is that it needs to be measurable and have a time frame attached to it. It also has to be attainable, even if you have to stretch to get there.

Here's my shot at setting some financial goals. You start with this:

My #1 financial goal after graduating college
and getting my first job is:

Then add what you think your goal is. Here's what my initial framework for a goal would look like:

My #1 financial goal after graduating college
and getting my first job is:

To immediately have a financial plan in place that helps me manage my day-to-day money goals, and my long-term financial goals, so that I can (accomplish something specific) _____ by (pick a date) _____.

Then you make it real by setting the goal and putting a deadline on it. Here are examples to fill-in those blanks:

1)...so that I can <u>save $1000 a month for my 6-month Emergency Fund and have it full</u> by <u>two years from today</u>.

2)...so that I can <u>save 5% of my gross income to payoff my student loans</u> by <u>ten years from today</u>.

3)...so that I can <u>put 10% of my gross income into a savings account and create an investment fund</u> by <u>three years from today</u>.

4)...so that I can save 15% of my gross income to build <u>up a $30,000 down payment to buy a new house</u> by <u>six years from today</u>.

Get out a clean sheet of paper and give it a try and see what you come up with.

Write this down first:

*My #1 financial goal after graduating college
and getting my first job is:*

Then start writing your goal down. Use the previous examples to get started. Just make sure that they genuinely work for you. It will be messy at first, so just keep at it until it starts making sense. Put it up on your wall as a reminder.

Once you have a well-defined goal with a time frame attached you can begin to focus on making it happen. You can have as many goals as you like just make sure they aren't in conflict with each other. Also make sure that you definitely have a date on the goal so that you can measure your success.

Chapter 23

~

The top financial goals of 650 of your fellow college students

Without goals, and ways to achieve them,
you are going to be going nowhere fast.

From 2008 to 2010, which was during the worst recession most of us have ever seen (aka: The Great Recession), I conducted research among 650 business majors from the University of Central Florida and the University of Washington. I chose these universities because they "book-ended" the country and each represented a mix of both liberal and conservative viewpoints and upbringings. I also had ready access to these two groups of students because both schools use one of my books in their business courses.

As you read in the previous chapter the single research question I asked was:

"What is your #1 financial goal after you graduate
and get your first job?"

It was a bit of a trick question, but I was trying to see if anyone was thinking about his or her own financial "big picture" plan first rather than singular goals.

Just 10 of the 650 people (1.5%) responded in a way that told me they "get it" when it comes to having some sort of a plan for their personal finances.

Here are their responses to my question:

> "To pay my mortgage & bills in *one* paycheck (out of two each month)."

> "Plan my spending and keep track of it so I don't have to worry about finances. I don't want to spend money that I don't have."

> "To keep building my savings account and keep building the portfolio that my mom started for me after high school. Also, to buy a house somewhere where the market is doing well."

> "To be able to afford all of my living expenses, pay off credit cards & have enough left over to begin saving & investing."

> "Save more than I spend and build wealth through wise investments."

> "Pay off all my debt, save money for a house, save for my retirement, and invest money."

> "To begin saving immediately. I will put money away for a house and retirement."

> "To be self-sufficient with a large amount of emergency money in the bank and lucrative investments to be able to retire early."

> "To save at least half of what I make & to start figuring out how much I need to save for retirement, kids, and to continue to be debt free."

> "Start a retirement fund since social security will be gone."

Those were enlightening responses, but the answer I was *really* looking for was that the students #1 financial goal was something like:

> *"To have a <u>financial plan</u>,*
> *before I do anything with my money."*

The above responses were as close as it got. That's not bad. The responses were not surprising because most of us focus on one thing at a time without first looking at how everything is interrelated. Maybe you'll think differently after reading this.

Take the goals that you came up with in the last chapter and see how they compare to research results from 650 of your fellow college peers in the next section. You can read this entire next chapter or just focus in on what is close to the financial goals you selected. After you've read the rest of this chapter check to see if there is anything you'd like to change about *your* financial goals. Go for it!

Here are the student responses to my question, broken down into three categories:

1. FINANCIAL GOALS

- 17.5% want to find a job with an annual average salary of $67,340
- 16.9% want to buy a house/condo
- 16.3% want to pay-off credit cards and student loans
- 10.0% want to start saving
- 8.6% want to start making investments
- 7.5% want to save for a house/condo
- 5.5% want to start saving for retirement
- 2.2% want to invest in real estate
- 2.2% want to invest in graduate school or their own business
- 1.4% want to be millionaires

2. FINANCIALLY GOOD INTENTIONS BUT VAGUE GOALS

- 17.8% had loose goals of living comfortably, having stable finances, paying their bills, etc.

Here is how those vague goals break down:

- 4.3% want to be able pay their bills
- 3.8% want to make money
- 3.5% want to make enough money to "live comfortably"

- 3.4% want to be financially independent/
  stable/secure
- Less than 1% each:
  Want to live below their means, Don't want
  to have to live paycheck to paycheck, Want to
  support their parents or family, Just want to
  survive, Want to be happy, and Want to build
  up their credit

3. NON-FINANCIAL GOALS

- 4.3% want to buy a car
- 2.2% want to buy things like a sailboat, toys,
guitar, etc.; "invest" in the lottery, buy a dog, or get
married

(Math Note: These percentages will add up to
more than 100% because many students gave
multiple responses to the question.)

~

Next, I'm going to analyze these responses and see how realistic
they are. I've also included some advice and things to think
about after my analysis.

1. FINANCIAL GOALS

**17.5% want to find a job with an average annual
salary of $67,340**

What's interesting about this response is that the students gave
a specific salary number as their goal. This is impressive and it
shows focus.

Everyone should be looking for a job unless they are going
to graduate school or doing volunteer work, so I debated
categorizing whether "finding a job" was a financial goal. But
because these students were specific about the amount they

were looking for I considered it a worthy goal. Income/cash flow is what fuels your economic engine initially so focusing on earning as much as you can is a good thing, as long as it's realistic.

As noted previously the average starting salary for a college student in 2010 was $48,351. The response from students who gave a specific number in this survey averaged out to $67,340. That's about 40% higher than the national average. Some of that can be explained by the fact that each school was located on a coast where the cost of living is typically higher. As I mentioned previously this was a group of business majors whose starting salaries typically skew higher, but not higher than most engineering jobs. As you will see later in the book, engineering jobs usually start at the highest initial salary levels.

While I admit that the students I polled were generally overachievers in business schools there is a potential disconnect here between salary reality and their expectations. This could be true for all college students in general.

You'll see from the Payscale.com list of *TOP 15 Median Salaries of First Year College Graduate Jobs for 2010-2011* (from pages 179-180) that $67,340 ranks just under the #1 top starting salary job: Petroleum Engineering. What this tells me is that graduating college seniors need to be more realistic in their salary goals – or at least maybe the business majors do. What I suggest here is that, in addition to getting a great job, beating that $48K average salary by a reasonable margin would be a more realistic goal.

> DON'T SPEND IT BEFORE YOU MAKE IT: Don't start spending your anticipated first year's salary before you know exactly what it is, and be wise about your spending once you do know what it is. Your earnings, spending, and ability to create wealth are all interconnected. A choice you make in one place will impact other areas.

16.9% want to buy a house/condo

When I saw how many students gave this response I wondered how many just wanted to do this because that's what their parents did or if they were responding to one of the *often-repeated myths* of the ages that has always said you should do this. If you buy a house or condo when you graduate you could be way ahead of the buying (and debt) curve for your age. That might not be a good thing. Any previous students who graduated in 2003-2008 and went right out and bought a house are most likely "underwater" on the value of their home today versus what they paid for it. That's not good.

According to a 2008 study from the National Association of Home Builders, first-time buyers were, on average, about 33 years old, had a household income of almost $64,100, bought a house with a median price of $150,000 and accounted for 43 percent of homes sold. If you buy a house at the $48K average college starting salary you might immediately start creating financial stress for yourself.

While buying a home right when you graduate is a noble goal, it may not be practical for many reasons:

1) If you have student loans you will be paying them off over 10-20 years depending on the loan type. At the 10-year mark, which is typical for most student loans, you will be approximately 33 years old, which coincides (but is no coincidence, I think?) with the age that most people buy their first home. Interesting.

2) You simply may not qualify for a loan under the more recent standards.

3) Owning a home immediately can limit your flexibility to move on to other geographical job opportunities. Homes are not "liquid" assets that can be easily sold these days. Owning a home also ties up a lot of money that could

be used for many other age appropriate shorter-term financial strategies. It can also make you house poor... meaning that so much money, as a percentage of your income, would be allocated to your home and related expenses that it could choke you financially. When I was just out of college my peers used to love to "happily" complain about being in this predicament. I always thought it was a dumb strategy - the complaining *and* the predicament.

CONSIDER THE 25% RULE: A good rule of thumb is to have no more than 25% of your gross salary dedicated to your housing bills, and that includes renting or owning. It could be a little higher when you buy and have an interest deduction. That percentage includes *all* your related housing bills...which means mortgage and taxes, or rent, insurance, utilities, repair fund, etc. Many real estate people will say to you: "In *this* market it's usually higher than 25%." Of course they will say that...

~

Many of the *often-repeated myths* of previous generations have to be rethought, like: You must buy a house ASAP! A home used to be considered an investment. These days a "home" is really a place to stay, and any real estate that throws off cash flow and income is considered a "true" investment.

With the economy the way it is these days, renting is more often a better approach if you are in your early 20's. If you follow the age averages and buy your first home at 33 you'll have about 10 years to save up a down payment and get adjusted financially. You'll also be much wiser about money by then, and less prone to many "first time buyer" mistakes.

What about buying that condo?

Condos "seem" like an inexpensive way to get into a home... right? Be careful. They get the same opinion from me that homes do...only it's worse. If you are considering a condo pay close attention to these things: Homeowner Association dues (they aren't tax deductible), your ability to sell if/when you want or need to move, assessments to cover repair costs and equipment failures, and snarky homeowner associations that are on power-trips.

There is also an excessive condo supply that some markets are experiencing these days. A lot of condo projects were converted to rental apartments when the real estate market collapsed. That's somewhat hidden inventory that could come back on the market at some point in the future and further drive down prices.

> HIDDEN COSTS: Also take note of the exterior construction methods used to build condos. For decades I have seen condos around the country that are only 5-10 years old with scaffolding around them to replace windows and siding that were improperly installed and sealed, and couldn't handle the climate. These repairs are expensive, sometimes more than the building cost to construct in the first place. Homeowners typically get assessed for the repair of these damages when building insurance doesn't cover the bills. It could be a very large and unwelcome financial surprise. I see this happening over an over again, so someone is either not paying attention or doesn't care.

Personally, I would opt for renting a small house before ever considering renting, or worse – buying, a condo. The latter are too restrictive with all their rules, regulations and monthly fees.

16.3% want to pay-off credit cards and student loans

It's interesting to note that while 16.9% of the students wanted to get into debt by buying a home immediately an almost equal amount, 16.3%, are trying to get out of debt by wanting to pay off their student loans and credit cards. Getting out of debt is the smarter strategy and will be for the foreseeable future.

I'd vote for getting out of credit card debt before getting deeply into housing debt. Many students today have financed a college housing lifestyle similar to what their parents once afforded them...and they've done it with student loans and credit cards. They probably shouldn't have. College housing costs are in addition to student loans for tuition and books. Credit over the last 5-10 years was pretty free flowing until the Great Recession hit. Now we are learning how to be more cash-based...just like the "good old days" which weren't all that long ago.

A plan for paying off your shortest term, highest interest debt first typically makes sense for creating a debt-free lifestyle. It helps you create total credit card pay-off momentum. Knock these cards off, as in - paid in full, one at a time and you'll relieve a lot of stress. Always pay off all your monthly bills in a timely manner so you can start to build up your credit and credit score.

10.0% want to start saving

This is an excellent response because frankly, I expected lower, but it should be more like 100%. Unfortunately, the thought of saving is incredibly boring for most. It bores me too, but then breathing is also boring. But if you aren't breathing then you're dead, and that's not good either, right? How does the thought of financial freedom and being able to do whatever you want while living within your means sound to you? That's much more exciting! And it all starts with saving.

At this point in your life the smartest thing you can do is to start putting away as much money as possible. Saving won't make you rich...especially at today's interest rates. That's not really the point though. Right now, for you, it's all about starting a great money related habit: Parking your money so you won't spend it frivolously while you are getting ready to take the next steps with it.

There's more on this later in the book but you start saving by creating an Emergency Fund. Don't ever touch it. After you've filled the Emergency Fund start saving to invest and there will be those proverbial "financially blue skies" ahead for you.

8.6% want to start making investments

This is a great idea, but not right now. I say this numerous times in the book: Only invest what you can afford to lose. Make that the next "tat" you put on your wrist or ankle. Right now you really can't afford to lose anything because you are just getting started.

The only investment that would make sense for you right now is a retirement account that your employer contributes to with matching dollars. There will be more about this ahead.

7.5% want to save for a house/condo

This makes much more sense than buying anything right now... for most people. As noted above, you've got 10 years before most former students will pay-off their student loans and buy their first house...so let that statistic work to your advantage.

It's true that there is potentially a lot of money to be made in the real estate market right now...but that is for an investor who has the funding, resiliency and patience to take advantage of any deals that are out there. The smart ones would already have their investment funds in place. You are really not ready for that yet.

The real estate market is still very messy and there will be years of inventory that needs to be "worked off" before it fully recovers, depending on your local market. Timing is everything when making real estate investments. Don't be tempted if you aren't financially stable yet. There will always be ways to make money in real estate, in the future.

5.5% want to start saving for retirement

It's gratifying that some students thought this was important. It becomes even more important, and less financially attainable the longer you wait. It's a great goal to start funding your retirement at an early age. A 401(k) is one of the few investments that you should think about making right now, especially if your employer is partially funding it with matching funds. Your contribution should be in the 5% range *for now*, plus whatever your employer contributes. You can always contribute more when you get raises.

> RECONSIDER MAXING-OUT YOUR 401(k): If you channel too much money into your retirement account – especially if your company doesn't fully match your 401(k) – you will be taking flexible investment money out of your hands and putting in a place where you can't get to it without paying a penalty, unless you make investments inside your retirement account – which can be tricky. The traditional *often-repeated myth* you will hear is to max out your 401(k). While I'm a fan of that in some cases, I'd rather have the ability to be a little more flexible with my money during the beginning of my career by putting it in places where I can have access to it, for smart investment purposes, and without penalties.

Which is better for you...a regular IRA or a Roth IRA?

You can have regular and Roth IRAs in addition to a 401(k). For the sake of simplicity I would try to have as few retirement plans as possible. For young people the 401(k) and a Roth IRA are a better deal.

Why? With a 401(k) you get a tax deduction on the amount you put in, plus you usually get that employer contribution. If your employer matches 50%-100% that is still more than what your tax rate will most likely be when you retire. Take that free money.

85

With the Roth IRA you end up paying taxes before you put the money into the account, but you pay no taxes on your earnings when you withdraw them during retirement. The maximum amount you can contribute to a Roth IRA is $5,000 annually before age 50. The Roth IRA is especially good when you are young because after a certain adjusted gross income level you can't make contributions, you would have to open a regular IRA to do that. For 2011, if you make over $122,000 (single) or $179,000 (married filing jointly) you can't contribute to a Roth IRA. That's probably not a problem for you...yet.

Between a 401(k) and a Roth IRA you get the most bang for your retirement bucks. But you only want to create these accounts as part of your overall financial plan.

2.2% want to invest in real estate

Investing in real estate is different than buying a home. Investing in just about anything isn't wise until you've built up an emergency fund and additional savings. Some investors currently see a "never seen before" opportunity in the real estate market. There will always be "never seen before" opportunities out there and some of them are even legit.

Unless the company you work for invests in distressed properties or flips real estate I wouldn't get involved in this personally at this point in your life. The timing is better for you to do so many other things right now, like getting established financially. Later down the road there will be opportunities to invest in real estate through REITs (Real Estate Investment Trusts).

I will add that any investments you make in the future (real estate or otherwise) should be well thought out and part of your overall financial plan.

2.2% want to invest in graduate school or their own business

I considered this to be a good investment goal because it was about a future personal success. In some respects it's really no different than investing in a start-up or the stock market because you are channeling resources into something that has the potential for big future gains. In this case it's an investment in human capital...you.

Because this would be an investment in "you" I would be OK with suspending my suggestion of "investing no more than you can afford to lose." Investing in you is a wise move, as long as you are making a smart investment in a career that will realistically increase your cash flow and net worth, while not getting yourself into too much debt.

> THE COST OF A CAREER RESTART: If you are doing a "restart" in your career, make sure you understand what that means to your ability to make a living. You will probably start towards the bottom rung of the corporate ladder.

Before you choose to invest more in yourself read the section at the end of the book entitled: "They probably didn't tell you this in high school" and apply it to where you are now in your life.

1.4% want to be millionaires

I took this response seriously when the poll results were being tabulated. There were a few "wise a$$" responses - but I tossed those as "outliers" like any good researcher would.

I consider wanting to be a millionaire a legit goal...even if the response was a little light on the details as to how that would happen and the time frame for it. You need to be creative and focused to get there, and it's hard to get there without stating what your goals are in some way. You need the right mind-set.

I was curious about how many people would respond with this answer. Around 1.4% is about the response rate that I'd expect from a projectable sample size of 650 people. Why? It mirrors the percentage of millionaires out in the real world.

Many people will off-handedly say that they want to be millionaires, but few will commit to it when seriously asked what their personal financial goals are.

Research shows that between 1-3% of the US population are millionaires, depending on which research study you use. So many people have the potential to be wealthy but just don't know how. If you can't think it, or dream it, you will never get there.

2. GOOD INTENTIONS BUT FINANCIALLY VAGUE GOALS

17.8% had goals of paying their bills, making money, living comfortably, being financially independent/stable/secure, etc.

This was the single largest group of answers but these "goals" will ultimately prove difficult to meet because they can't be measured. They were vague but at least they had positive thoughts about their financial goals.

If your goal is to "pay your bills" does that mean: Pay them off? Pay them on time? Pay them when you feel like it? Create higher bills than you should but still stretch to pay them?

If your goal is to "live comfortably" does that mean: Being able to always make the mortgage payment that you might have forever? Or, paying off all your long-term financial commitments and then retiring?

The lesson learned here is that the more specific you can be when setting a goal the easier it will be to achieve it. None of the "goals" below pass that test, but they make for an interesting discussion.

Here are some of the vague goals that the students stated:

4.3% want to pay their bills

This type of thinking is a potentially great start, but you have to be specific about how you are going to do it.

A good goal would be to say: "My goal is to minimize my monthly bills and pay them on time each month." That meets the test of a good goal: a specific task and a time frame to accomplish it.

3.8% want to make money

Their heart is in the right place with this response, but they won't get there if they aren't more specific. How do they want to make money? How much? Over what time frame?

A good goal here might be: "To make more money than all my bills combined and have $300 to put in my savings account at the beginning of each month." There are many other ways to make this statement into a realistic goal.

3.5% want to make enough money to "live comfortably"

I'm not sure exactly what "live comfortably" means, how about you? It sounds like an underachiever goal to me, but it's no doubt well-intentioned. Does it mean that you get to drink a beer every night, eat out twice a week and call your life "comfortable"? For some people...maybe.

It's one of those "if I make some money life is going to be soooo easy" answers that sounds nice but seems to lack any specificity or time frame.

A good goal here might be: "To make enough money to pay all my bills on time each month and build a financial portfolio that would allow me to live my life with a substantial monetary cushion and retire when I'm 55 years old." Even that one is still a little vague, but it's heading in the right direction.

3.4% want to be financially independent/stable/secure

I think most people would naturally fall into this category. The question is: How do you get to be financially independent and how do you know when you've arrived in the land of stability? That's just one more example about why you need to be specific about your goals.

A good goal here might be similar to the one above, or: "To minimize my monthly bills and maximize my savings and investments so that I have amassed a net worth of $1 million by the time I am 45 years old." That has all the elements of a good, measurable goal.

Less than 1% each responded with the following:

Want to live below their means, Don't want to have to live paycheck to paycheck, Want to support their parents or family, Just want to survive, Want to be happy, and Want to build up their credit

As a group I'd say that these are all great mottoes to live by, and some could be turned into goals if some specifics and time frames were added.

3. NON-FINANCIAL GOALS

There were a few "goals" that popped-up that were clearly not financial goals in my estimation. I need to call these out so that people don't mislead themselves.

4.3% want to buy a car

Let's be clear here, buying a car is not a financial goal. It is a personal goal that needs to be financed. Three times more people gave this answer than those who said their #1 financial goal was to be a millionaire. That's troublesome, but it's also indicative of the lack of understanding that many people have about money and personal finances. And, I'm not just referring to college students.

A car is an expense, a depreciating asset, and a way to get from Point A to Point B. It might also be a nice reward for a major accomplishment later in life. If your post-college universe revolves solely around what car you are going to buy next and impressing your friends with it...well, you are going to have a disappointing life ahead of you because that mentality only gets worse with age. Ask me how I know.

2.2% want to buy things like a big sailboat, electronic toys, a guitar, etc.; invest in the lottery; buy a dog; or get married

Buying things is never considered a financial goal unless those "things" can make you a lot more money than they cost. Otherwise they are hobbies, not financial goals. I don't think that's where these respondents were coming from though. I can see where they might have been confused as they were answering. They might have meant that they want to be so successful that they can buy a "big sailboat". But the argument falls apart when someone answers: "Invest in the lottery!" That's never a good idea. Ever.

Buy a dog? Seriously? That's a financial goal? What about a cat?

And as a former girlfriend, who is a women's personal finance coach, once said to me, "A man is not a financial plan." I'll add that a woman isn't either! While getting married may be a life goal it certainly isn't a financial goal.

For what it's worth, many people recommend learning how to live on your own and pay your own bills for a while before ever considering moving in with someone or getting married. That's very smart advice.

Chapter 24

~

20 ways real life can impact your financial life

You earn money.
Then you spend it all.
Now what?

The decisions you make early in your life will travel along with you forever, so you'll want to make them carefully, right? Of course. You should live life to the fullest and have fun, but also realize all your choices have a financial impact, and you have to weigh them all fully before proceeding ahead.

That means you should know the real cost of things before you make a move. According to Wikipedia, J.P. Morgan uttered these infamous words:

"If you have to ask the price, you can't afford it."

It was in response to a question about how much his yachts cost to maintain. If you are super wealthy you might think a comment like that is funny. If you are like the rest of us, or you're super wealthy and actually care about how your money is being spent, that same comment sounds totally idiotic. Wanting to know what things cost before committing to them doesn't show a lack of wealth, it shows common sense.

Buying something without knowing the costs first is what gets many people into trouble financially. This is just another example of the kind of *often-repeated myths* that so many people can't seem to erase from their memory...yet this thinking rules many buying decisions. People just go out and buy what they want and deal with the bills, and related aftermath, later.

So what can get in the way of all the potential wealth that you could create during your lifetime? Two words: *real life*...and the choices you make while living it. Part of what we'll discuss in this section will help you avoid some of the pitfalls that may hurt your chances at having a financial safety net throughout your life.

Do what you want to do in life (legally), and know what your choices will cost before you make you them.

Here are 20 examples of life costs:

1. Hey, let's go out and party tonight! – Some people have a hard time breaking free of their college ways. And who doesn't like to go out every once in a while? Once people get a paycheck, those who aren't particularly good at managing their money can find plenty of ways to spend it quickly. In many cases it's in a bar, restaurant, show or sports event.

You pay for all the fun you have now with real money, not your college meal card. It all starts to add up...fast. Just take a look at your credit card bill when it comes in next time. Or take a look at the number of times you go to the ATM machine to get some "Teller Machine Fun Tickets" (=$20 bills). Don't pitch the receipts in the trash...keep an eye on them. They might help make a convincing point later.

One way to compromise on the "have fun now vs. save for future fun" strategy is to take advantage of happy hours. You can have a drink (if you drink) and some food on the cheap, so why not just consider it dinner? Then you can move on to more important things. You can also find no cost ways to go out and have a good time. It's the getting together with your friends that matters, not maxing-out your credit card and sending yourself into financial oblivion.

2. Text, text, text, yap, yap, yap...crash...ooops! – I hate to say this my friend, but your generation is notorious for thinking they can multitask. USNews.com has reported that 66% of those aged 18-24 say they have sent text messages from behind the wheel of a car. According to a Harris Interactive poll, 9 out of 10 adults believe that sending text messages or e-mails while driving is "distracting, dangerous, and should be outlawed." I doubt this is a generational issue; it's more like a common sense issue.

Here's a cold hard stat for you: Distracted driving (aka: texting and talking on your cell phone) kills over 5,500 people and injures over 450,000 more each year in the US each year. That's according to the US Department of Transportation. In the state of Florida there are over 600 accidents a day – or one about every 2 minutes – that are attributed to distracted driving. How much proof do you need to change your habits? Would one of your friends dying help make the point? Sadly, it probably wouldn't for a lot of people.

It's been proven that texting and driving don't mix. In fact it gives you a response time that is multiples worse than if you were 80 years old *and* driving drunk. Is it really worth it? Or put another way: Is an OMG-LOL text message worth dying for, or killing other people for? Can't that text message wait? Seriously. WTF! Don't think it can't happen to you. It can. And it does.

If you wreck a car and everyone walks away that's one thing. If you wreck another person's life, that's entirely worse. Either way, you will be paying for the financial consequences for some time. You will pay an insurance deductible if you cause a wreck, the other party will sue you, and you'll pay a premium on top of your insurance for years. That's providing you don't get dropped. Are you prepared for any of that?

Distracted driving laws are just starting to make their ways onto the books in many states. Don't wait for a law to tell you what common sense is.

What will driving distracted cost you? For states that have laws, and enforce them, there are hefty fines of over $100. States are now making the move towards assessing points on your license as well. More points = higher insurance premiums. Believe it or not, there used to be days when people just drove their cars and didn't have any distractions.

It won't kill you to not use your cellphone while you are driving, but if you do, it just might. Don't drive distracted. It could cost you more than just a lot of money. YOU. COULD. DIE.

3. Drinking or doing drugs...while driving = FAIL! – What is as bad, or worse, than distracted driving? Drinking or drugging, and driving, of course. A DUI/DWI can cost you a lot of money. It can also cost lives, maybe even yours. A DUI/DWI offense is not at all funny or excusable. Only reality stars think it is. It's also not just a "dumb mistake"...it's totally stupid and those that do it, even if they don't get caught, have serious problems with good judgment. Despite the obvious concerns the roads around colleges and universities are full of blue and red flashing lights and the sounds of zip-tie handcuffs being constantly applied to the wrists of drunken undergraduates. I guess we all think we are invincible at that age. We aren't.

According to MSNMoney.com here's what an average DUI costs: Bail $150-$2,500+, Towing $100-$1,200, Insurance surcharge $4,500+ (not including your regular auto insurance costs), Legal fees $2,000-$25,000. Also factor in: the ticket that will be issued, not being allowed to rent a car, the possibility of losing your job, and the fact that it will be on your record for years. It's not worth it. Be the designated driver or take a taxi. Never let someone who is drunk drive you anywhere...even if they say they are OK. You know they aren't.

4. Hanging out with losers – I'm not trying to be judgmental here, but sometimes the people you hang out with can affect your personal finances. Make sure that you know exactly what kind of people your friends really are. This includes: casual friends, regular friends and boyfriends or girlfriends. Do they have criminal records that they haven't told you about? Do they have bad credit? Are they a con artist? Is their past a big secret? Any/all of the above? If yes, they can potentially cost you a ton of money in lost personal loans, presumed guilt by association with them (from judgmental people anyway), a ruined reputation, identity theft (yours!), etc. Never loan money to losers. (And you should rarely lend money, even to friends.) Don't let them convince you to do things you shouldn't be doing or spending money you don't want to spend.

Here's an example of what hanging out with losers can cost you:

According to mashable.com, the average cost of an identity theft is $4,841. That's the equivalent of three months salary for the average worker. That doesn't include all the hassle of reclaiming your identity and dealing with the authorities and your bank. Add in another $851-$1,378 in out-of-pocket costs to resolve identity theft damage. About 1 in 10 American consumers have been victims of identity theft. Here's the really bad news: 43% of the victims knew the perpetrator who stole their identity.

Bad people can do all types of crafty things when it comes to separating you from your money. Here are some hints: Are they being overly friendly, generous or helpful on insignificant things? Once they befriend you do they start hinting that times are tough and they need money? Do they start suggesting that you invest in things you really don't know that much about? Are they asking a lot of questions about how much the things you have cost and about your personal finances and family money background? Are they introducing you to other people who also seem shady? If they know you've done well and are smart with money it's fine to give them casual advice, but don't discuss your personal finances openly with anyone but your financial advisor or trusted mentors who you are extremely close to. If you are really nervous about how someone is acting then don't hesitate to run a background check. If it's gotten that far you may want to trust your senses and find a new friend.

One of the biggest reasons we continue to hang out with losers is that we have some kind of insecurities that drive us to put up with more than we realistically should. Maybe we think we can't find better friends or that there is something wrong with us and we should give the other person a chance. Maybe we just feel sorry for the other person. You really have to fight these feelings and do the right thing...and that usually means to move on, as quickly and politely as you can. Getting rid of a loser in your life can set you free.

5. Investing in friends – Money and friendships shouldn't be mixed unless you have legal protections in place. Investing in a friend's company is totally legit if it's done with legal protections. Even then it's not always a great idea. Get plenty of advice from your mentors before proceeding down this path. Make sure it's a sound business investment and that you aren't being convinced just because you have a friendship with someone. I can't give you a specific number here...all I can tell you is losing a $1,000 investment is just as painful to some people as it is for others who lose $10,000 or $100,000. It's no fun when it's lost and has to become a write-off. I've been burned on this a few times. If it seems too good to be true...well, you know how this sentence ends.

6. Over-consuming – When I was a kid my Mom used to say: "Don't have eyes bigger than your stomach." That was usually said right before a family meal, especially one that we might be having out in a nice restaurant. The wisdom was clear: "Don't over do it on the consumption or you'll get a stomach ache."

Today, my Mom's message easily extends to the idea of having "eyes bigger than our wallets." There are a lot of people getting financial stomach aches these days. Americans are great over-consumers of lots of things, like: food, fancy cars, booze, big houses, drugs, infomercial junk, vacations, gambling, clothes, etc. We often can't stop. If you didn't have any of that stuff could you still be happy in life? That's probably another book for me to write.

If you over-consume on stuff/junk
you can become a broke hoarder.
If you over-consume on food you can get fat.
If you over-consume on booze you can get a
DUI/DWI and a lifetime membership to AA.
If you over-consume on drugs you can get killed.
None of this is good and it all costs you a lot of money.

The interesting thing about over-consuming financially is that it doesn't require credit cards to do it, though they do make it easier as you will see below in the credit card section. Any other form of money will do: check, cash, debit card, home equity line of credit, your 401(k), your investments, your kid's piggy bank, or worse, their college fund. You name it. If some people can find it, they can usually find a way to spend it.

The personal financial messes that people get into are mostly self-inflicted. Many people like to blame slick marketing and other external factors for their own mistakes. That might be true to a point, but no one is making you sign a sales contract, or pull out the credit card, except you. Each case is individual, so it's hard to put a number on what kind of mayhem something like over-consuming can do to your financial life. Just realize that if you find better role models you can greatly decrease your chances of succumbing to over-consumption.

7. Credit Cards – It might seem odd that credit cards would show up in the "life" portion of the book but they are the part of life that get many people in trouble. Many people charge all of their life expenses on a credit card. They are financing their life with excessive double-digit interest rates.

There is nothing wrong with credit cards, until they are used unwisely. Such is true with many things in life, right? Spending more than you have and making the minimum payments are what can get you in trouble fast. It all adds up so quickly that it can blind-side you. Recent changes in credit card finance rules require credit card companies to show you, on your monthly statement, what happens when you only make the minimum and how long it will take to pay-off your outstanding balance. You might want to pay very close attention to that math when you get that next statement.

According to creditcard.com the average credit card balance is almost $16,000. The average Annual Percentage Rate (APR) on those credit cards is over 14%. Additionally, 36% of those credit card holders don't know what their credit card interest rate is. Do you? All of those data points put together are a recipe for financial disaster.

It was reported that towards the end of 2010 consumer spending using credit cards was up a few percentage points, and savings percentages were down. Didn't we learn anything from the Great Recession? Apparently not, and that is crazy! Just because others charged their holiday spending, or are simply charging more in general, doesn't mean that you need to do what they are doing. The fact that "others are doing it" doesn't mean it's right, or smart. Don't follow the herd mentality. Remember, herds can become hamburger.

Do you know how long it would take to pay off your credit card balance while making the minimum payment?

Here's a quick way to do the math:

1. Take your outstanding credit card balance and divide it by the minimum payment. Let's say you owe $2,500. Your minimum payment is around 1.5% or $37. Guess who sets this? The credit card companies do! That equals approximately 68 payments (= over 5.6 years) assuming you stop using the card and always pay it on time.

But that's not all the math you need to know...

2. The previous example doesn't include the 29.99% annual interest penalty rate if you miss a payment, or even the typical "regular" interest rate of around 16.99% if you are paying on time. Those rates are charged against the unpaid balance. So as a rough calculation, add another 17% or 30% to the outstanding balance *at the beginning of each year* and keep dividing by that minimum payment.

Bottom Line: It will be way more than 68 payments to get that card paid off. OUCH! That will hurt. And that was just for an outstanding balance of $2,500!

Now you know why credit card companies love "minimum" payments. They maximize the amount of interest (= profit) they will make off you. Don't fall for the minimum payment scam. Yes, I consider it a scam. You are never told what all those interest rate charges will add up to. It may end up being multiples more than the cost of all the stuff you charged on the card and have already forgotten about.

Here's some good news:

According to the *2008 Student Monitor Annual Financial Services Study*, 41% of college students have a credit card. Of the students with cards, about 65% pay their bills in full every month, which is higher than the general adult population. For those of you that are paying off your monthly balance, keep up the good work! You truly get it. Just make sure you keep getting it.

Now let's fast-forward a few years. What happens when you have a family?

According to research done by demos.org, entitled *"Borrowing to Make Ends Meet"* (2007), the credit card statistics start to change for the worse. The average credit card-indebted family in 2004 allocated 21% of its income to servicing monthly debt compared to the 13% dedicated to debt payments among all households. I read that as 20% of someone's INCOME is going to pay for FINANCE charges. That's whacked. And you can't even write-off consumer interest any longer. This could point to the fact that people are unaware of what having and raising a family costs, and instead of paying on a cash basis they simply "charge-it." Uh-oh.

And what about debit cards?

They sure look like a credit card but, as you know, the money is zapped right out of your account. You get no ability to pay off the card at the end of the month because your purchases are "debited" to your account immediately. If you are an active debit card user you must know what's in your account at all times. As with credit cards, consider a debit card as cash - which it truly is - and don't spend more of it than you have available. Overcharging on a debit card generates a whole new level of profitability for banks: overdraft charges. Your bank will "own you" at that point and you will become a slave to high interest rates and excessive fees for a long, long time.

8. Homes & Mortgages – Seems like everyone will have a home and a mortgage at some point in their life. They aren't the "investment" they used to be. As mentioned previously, never buy more "home" than you can realistically afford. A large home and a large mortgage can sink your finances – especially if you use an Adjustable Rate Mortgage that continues to move up the payments over time. They are a really bad idea.

Also realize there are ongoing maintenance costs involved with any kind of home you buy – especially in older homes. And, know that in addition to the cost of the house there is the cost of financing the house. That cost is usually the same as the principal: a $200,000 house will usually cost around $200,000 to finance over 30 years at today's interest rates – that's a total cost of $400,000).

9. Engagement – Here's another example of those *often-repeated myths* that people have been mindlessly saying for years. It's a classic and it goes like this: "You must spend two to three months salary on an engagement ring." Sound familiar? Guess who came up with that idea? The De Beers Diamond marketing people, of course! It became a rule of thumb for decades for clueless guys who wanted to marry that cute girl they just couldn't get enough of. Hopefully we've evolved past this kind of "2-3 months ring rule" thinking, but that change happens slowly for most. You still hear otherwise intelligent people saying it today.

You should spend whatever you can realistically afford for an engagement ring. Some couples don't think an engagement ring is even necessary...the concept does date back to the 13th Century after all. (Source: Wikipedia.) That's *very* old school.

Team up with your significant other and go through the "ring" process together. You will learn a lot about each other's perspective on money. And, surprising your significant other with an engagement ring can also create all kinds of unintended financial surprises.

So, what do you do about "the ring?" Get creative. Be unique. Find a cool antique ring...diamond or otherwise. Maybe even one that has been in your family for years. It worked for Prince William and Kate Middleton. He gave her his mother's engagement ring whose primary stone wasn't even a diamond.

If your significant-other-to-be is just as money conscious as you are, but still wants a ring, maybe they'd be thrilled to have a large *flawless* synthetic (man-made) diamond in the family because it truly defines "perfection." And it would be more fun to flaunt to any shallow friends, of course. You could both put the rest of the money in the bank as a down payment on a house a few years after you get married. You never know until you both discuss it. It's just an idea.

I hate to go on and on about this...but I find it fascinating. Here's the interesting thing about man-made diamonds: They are real diamonds. They are flawless, meaning they have no inclusions.

To get an almost perfect, yet not-really-perfect, diamond that is mined out of the ground you have to pay a fortune. This makes no sense to me. But here's the second case in our engagement discussion of not being able to break free from all the *often-repeated myths* of the past.

According to lovetoknow.com the range for engagement rings is $200-$20,000+, with the average cost of an engagement ring being between $3,500-$4,000. The sources of a lot of this information are jewelers and the diamond industry...so what do you expect the average to be...lower maybe?

And don't think that the size of the diamond is any guarantee that people will stay married longer. These days people can't be "guilt-tripped" into staying married longer if they don't want to be, no matter how big their "rock" is.

Also know that, according to Wikipedia: Engagement rings are typically considered "conditional gifts" and only become property of the woman if the marriage happens. Most states today use a no-fault rule so that it doesn't matter who breaks the engagement, the ring usually goes back to the man.

Oh, and good luck selling that ring for what you paid for it. For being as valuable, allegedly timeless, and rare as diamonds are supposed to be, the only time it has full retail value is when it is appraised and when a jeweler sells it to someone. Maybe that's the third *often-repeated myth* that needs to be blown-up.

Now, here's a fourth *often-repeated myth*: Diamonds are rare. Really? If diamonds are so rare, why are there so many of them?

10. Not having a pre-nuptial agreement – Some people believe in pre-nuptial agreements and some don't. I'm willing to guess that anyone unfortunate enough to deal with a divorce - you'll see the stats in the Divorce section - wishes they had one after the fact. It's often said that the quickest way to lose half of your net worth is not by being in the stock market...it's by getting divorced.

With young people getting married a little later in life these days
- for women it's around 25, for men it's around 27, according to
the Minneapolis Star Tribune (startribune.com) - you will have
personal assets and possibly family assets that you'll want to
protect. Trust me, you don't want to be giving away half of the
family beach house when you get divorced. Ask me how I know.

It will rarely matter during the divorce proceedings if one
person in a relationship is the saver and one is the spender. In
most states you each get half of the assets, unless something
has been negotiated in advance, and that's where a pre-nuptial
agreement comes in. It doesn't seem too fair if you're the saver
and your significant other is the big spender, and you have to
give up half of your combined estate...does it? This is especially
true if you have to give up family assets.

When you are young, and you and your new spouse are
essentially starting with very little, a pre-nuptial agreement
might not seem to make sense. It seems counter-intuitive to
"true love." But, what happens if you receive an inheritance
or that Internet company you went to work for - or started -
becomes a huge hit...and then you get a divorce? There are
plenty of great financial scenarios that can happen to you when
you are young.

The things I hear over and over from people that marry young
and then get divorced are: "I was too young." "I changed and
they didn't." "They (the other person) spent all our money."
And, the ever popular, "They cheated on me." No one ever thinks
these things can happen to *them*. Until they do.

Here's one way to look at the importance of pre-nuptial
agreements: In the eyes of the state your marriage is a business
contract. In the eyes of whatever religion you practice, if any, it
may be a moral contract or something else. It's also about an
emotional connection, which makes it more difficult when you
get divorced.

RE-THINKING PRE-NUPS: If someone proposed a business investment to you that you knew in advance had a 50% chance of failure, and you still chose to invest because the returns could be great, would you enter into a business agreement like that with no legal protection? I didn't think so.

Pre-nuptial agreements are similar. They end up being a road map to what a relationship looks like if it unfortunately has to end. Everyone knows how they will be treated, in theory, and how they will be taken care of. In some respects it's a form of "insurance," or maybe that word should be "assurance." When all the emotions are swirling around in a divorce it's nice to have some idea of how it will all settle out.

Pre-Nuptial Agreements should always be reviewed by a separate attorney representing each party individually, and done at least 4-6 months in advance of getting married. My recommendation is that the significant other have a "better" attorney than the person suggesting the Pre-Nuptial Agreement.

11. Marriage – Marriage is a fine institution, and one that costs a lot of money to enter into. The average cost of a wedding according to the Association for Wedding Professionals International is $21,000-$24,000. I've been to weddings that were 10 times less expensive and 10 times more expensive.

One question many couples don't ask is: "Who are we doing this wedding for: Us or our friends and family?" Some people choose to do smaller more creative ceremonies at a lower cost or they simply elope and have a nice party upon their return. They put the rest of the money towards their financial plan. Others choose to be together but not married. The choice is yours, but know what the costs are.

Also consider the timing of getting married. No, not so you can get a tax deduction (OK, maybe...but), it's more like this: If you are a financial mess or you intend to marry someone who also is, your financial future won't get any brighter. It will probably get worse. Both potential spouses should have their financial act together before even coming close to walking down the aisle. Ask me how I know.

Your financial compatibility is just as important as all the other compatibility issues you will need to be in agreement with. Whatever seems to be a little issue before you get married always becomes magnified after you get married, especially when it comes to money. Suggest to your significant other that you both run credit reports and FICO scores and get them cleaned up if they are in bad shape. If your significant other doesn't like that idea then that's a tip that there is something they don't want you to know. Think long and hard about how much you'd want to be married to someone like this.

12. Having kids – Kids are great, for most people. They are also costly. Don't consider having them with financial blinders on. Many people will say that kids are worth every cent they "invest" in them, while others aren't so sure. I'll leave that decision to you, but here's the financial aspect:

First, what's the cost of delivering a baby?

Actually, it appears that costs are all over the map. It depends greatly on where in the country you are located, if you are insured or not, and if it's a normal birth or a C-section.

Costhelper.com provides the following information:

> "For patients not covered by health insurance, the typical cost of a normal delivery without complications ranges from about $9,000 to $17,000 or more, depending on geographic location and whether there is a discount for uninsured patients.

The typical cost for a C-section without complications, or a normal delivery with complications, ranges from about $14,000 to $25,000 or more."

"For patients with insurance, out-of-pocket costs usually range from under $500 to $3,000 or more, depending on the plan. Out-of-pocket expenses typically include co-pays - usually $15 to $30 for a doctor visit and about $200 to $500 for inpatient services for delivery. Some insurance plans only cover a percentage - usually about 80 to 90 percent after a deductible is met, so you can easily end up reaching your yearly out-of-pocket maximum. In most plans, that ranges from about $1,500 to $3,000."

AND GET THIS: "Usually, the baby receives a separate bill, which typically ranges from $1,500 to $4,000 for a healthy baby delivered at term. For a premature baby with complications who has to spend weeks in a neonatal intensive care unit, this bill can reach tens of thousands of dollars."

It's ironic that within hours of being born a child is already in debt for his or her own birth. Yes, in many cases the child gets a medical bill separate from the parents. Welcome to America... now pay-up! Or better yet, finance it!

I've also read with great curiosity that one family was so overwhelmed by the medical bill for the birth of their son: $30,000 in costs to them (and that's *with* insurance) that they had to file bankruptcy.

Note that the above are delivery costs only, and do not include prenatal care that would include ultrasounds, and other tests, etc. Yes, it's expensive.

Having unexpected costs when having a child can disrupt the "new parent" experience for more than just the short term. It pays to know what the full range of costs could be before you decide to get pregnant, not right before you are going to have the baby.

Second, what about the cost of raising those children?

According to MSNMoney.com, for couples that earn $56,670 to $98,120 a year it costs an average of $222,000 to raise a child from birth to age 17. That does not include college costs.

If that $222,000 looks like too unrealistic (= too big) of a number for you then think of it in monthly terms. The average is just under $1,100 a month...though your costs will be nowhere near average on a monthly basis. Do you have an extra $1,100 a month to support a child? It all starts adding up from before day one and you need to budget for it, in advance.

13. Your kid's college – According to collegeboard.com the average cost of a four-year public university education in 2010 was $7,605/year for in-state student tuition and fees. For private institutions tuition and fees jump to $27,293/year. For two-year colleges the average tuition and fees are $2,713/year. These are "full retail" prices and don't include grants, scholarships or financial aid.

None of the above amounts include room, board or books. They also don't include the interest you'd pay on student loans for 10-20 years. It is difficult, if not impossible, to estimate what tuition will cost in 20+ years when many people who graduate college today will be sending their kids off to college. One thing you should know is that it won't be inexpensive.

If you are planning on having children at some point you'll want to start researching the 529 Plans that will one day fund your children's education. What this all means is that you'll need to start putting money away for that...as soon as your children are born. Funding a 529 Plan should always come after you've funded your Emergency Fund, contributed to your retirement fund and made any debt repayments that you are responsible for. Once you've checked-out the facts on 529 Plans remind your kids to think "good grades" and "scholarship" whenever possible.

> A GREAT EDUCATION INVESTMENT IDEA: This might work if you ever send kids off to college. Before I went off to college my Dad struck what I thought was a fair deal with me. Dad said that he and Mom would invest in me if I would invest in me. That meant they would pay for my college and expenses and I would pay them back half of it later when I was able. That certainly motivated me to get a lot out of my education. There was no set time frame or interest rate for repayment, which works well if you trust your kids. The deal made total sense to me. In addition to their support I got scholarships and worked a few jobs to lighten their financial load. I ultimately paid them back 100% as fast as I could because I wanted to be a good investment for them. It worked out well for everyone.

14. Divorce – According to the US Census Bureau 50% of marriages end in divorce, with the average first marriage lasting 8 years. There are many reasons why people get divorced. It's not always about the money, even though that's one of the top reasons...but it probably will be about the money when the divorce process starts.

A divorce costs money...lots of money. According to ehow.com the cost of an uncontested divorce is around $1,500 (I'm not sure I believe that number...). According to USNews.com the cost of a mediated divorce is less than $7,000, while a collaborative divorce is less than $20,000. The cost of a contested divorce is around $27,000. Nasty divorces can cost $78,000 or a lot more. These amounts do not include alimony and childcare, which can go on for years and be very expensive. They also don't include the cost of accountants and private investigators, etc. So it seems that getting divorced can cost a lot more than getting married. Your mileage may vary.

You also need to factor in the "other" costs of divorce such as moving, health care and paying for your children's education.

15. Personal Bankruptcy – Bankruptcy is one thing you never want to have to deal with. It's complicated and it's expensive. Do you file Chapter 7 or 13? When? How? There are filing fees (around $275-$300), accountant and witness fees (that $$$ amount is open ended) and lawyer expenses ($1,000 - $3,500+). Plus, a bankruptcy lasts on your credit reports for 10 years max and that limits your ability to borrow money or get a home mortgage. Bankruptcies are also public information and employers can look at them during the hiring and promotion process.

According to bankrate.com and howitworks.com the different types of bankruptcy are:

Chapter 7: This is a personal, consumer form of bankruptcy. You will be able to walk away from most of your debt relatively quickly, after your assets have been liquidated. You keep your paycheck, but the bankruptcy stays on your credit report for 10 years, and you are a higher risk than a Chapter 13 so you get hit with higher fees and interest rates.

Chapter 13: Personal businesses typically use this form of bankruptcy. You will be paying off some of your debts over a 3-5 year reorganization plan, the court sets how much you get to live on, and your trustee pays your creditors with your money. It stays on your credit report for the balance of the 10-year period.

In both cases you have to work hard to re-establish credit immediately.

In most situations you are not released from your student loan obligations unless you pass an "undue hardship" test. And that's rare. The courts also look at your behavior in the bankruptcy process. Have you been re-paying your student loans for a while? Are the loan payments keeping you from living at a minimum standard? Just because you think your education was "too expensive" or you "don't feel like paying the money back" are not good excuses to file bankruptcy.

Avoid bankruptcy at all costs. Period. The lawyers who advertise on TV make it sound easy and painless...it's far from that.

What about "strategic defaults"? Ever heard of them?

There is an alarming trend today that will more likely affect people in your parents age group than you...for now. It happens when people who can still pay their home loans (or not) choose to walk away when the amount owed is significantly higher than the current value of the home. While it doesn't necessarily require a bankruptcy (that depends on the state) it does mess up your credit for a long time. I come from the school of thought that if you sign up for a loan to buy something then you have a moral obligation to actually pay-off any loan you have signed for. What you choose to do is, of course, up to you.

16. Poor Health – Poor health can cost you a lot of money. USAToday.com reports that: According to government data, about 66% of people in the USA (in 2007) were either overweight or obese. According to associatedcontent.com (a Yahoo site), the Center for Disease Control (CDC) puts estimated medical costs of obesity and associated disease treatment at around $147 billion annually, and that cost is expected to rise. Who do you think pays for all that? The answer isn't the government. It's you and me.

You can't eliminate all your health risks, but you can do your best to stay healthy. That includes eating healthy, exercising, and not smoking, drinking excessively, or doing drugs. Bad health can wipe you out and cause bankruptcy. The majority of personal bankruptcies in the US are medical expense related.

Businessweek.com reported in 2007 that: "Medical problems caused 62% of all personal bankruptcies filed in the U.S., according to a study by Harvard researchers. And in a finding that surprised even the researchers, 78% of those filers had medical insurance at the start of their illness, including 60.3% who had private coverage, not Medicare or Medicaid."

Additionally, according to a health.com study (2007) covered by CNN: "62.1% of bankruptcies are medically related because the individuals had more than $5,000 (or 10 percent of their pretax income) in medical bills, mortgaged their home to pay for medical bills, or lost significant income due to an illness. On average, medically bankrupt families had $17,943 in out-of-pocket expenses, including $26,971 for those who lacked insurance and $17,749 who had insurance at some point"

And, it's not just the cost of health care (underinsured or uninsured) that can affect your finances. According to the National Bureau of Economic Research, the top third of the "health distribution" curve, meaning those in good health, had accumulated 50% more in assets than those in the bottom third of the curve, or those in bad health.

Make it your personal health goal
to stay out of the emergency room.

Take every opportunity to stay in shape and maintain your health, and health insurance. No one is going to "take care of you" when it comes to your health. The concept of personal responsibility is especially important here.

I don't want to make this a political discussion, but do we wonder why the First Lady has made childhood obesity the center of her attention? Some political pundits will say that the government shouldn't tell people what to eat. Well, its pretty clear that the majority of Americans have no self-control over what they put in their mouths...since two thirds are overweight or obese. So maybe most people do need a little guidance?

112

Despite the "diet industry" being an almost $60 billion - yes, that's with a "b" – it's pretty clear that diets in their present forms do not work. Exercise and changes to sedentary lifestyles are what's needed...there is no magic silver bullet that is going to save people from themselves.

Accumulating good health is more important than accumulating great wealth, but you increase your chances of maintaining your wealth when you work to keep your health.

17. Smoking – Smoking is costly in many aspects. According to MSNMoney.com the cost of smoking includes: cigarettes, dry cleaning, house cleaning, car cleaning, breath fresheners and health insurance. And, many companies won't hire smokers. When I last checked, the cost of cigarettes alone is expensive; they average $5.50 a pack nationally, a hefty $7.00+ per pack in Washington State and $11 per pack in New York.

MSNMoney.com estimates that a 40-year-old who quits and puts the savings into a 401(k) could save almost $250,000 by age 70. It's obviously even more when you stop smoking at a much younger age.

There's a range of costs to the actual "quitting" part of smoking. It can be $0 if you simply go "cold turkey" but the chances of staying smoke free are low. There are options that include: computer-based programs, hypnosis, nicotine gum, patches, nasal sprays and inhalers, and anti-smoking drugs. These programs can go for 8-to-24 weeks and can cost in the low $100's of dollars to $1000's of dollars. The actual cost depends on the smoking cessation program selected. Not all solutions work for everyone and success rates aren't stellar in my estimation. The better solution is to not start smoking to begin with. Then think how rich you'd be.

Smart people choose not to smoke for good reasons: The costs are high, it adds no value to your health, and it's perceived as a poor life choice. Think about it.

18. Addictions – Drug and alcohol addictions can cost you your money, career, and life. According to the website Drug-Rehabs. com, the cost of being addicted is expensive. Over a 20-year period the estimated costs of being addicted to these drugs are: Cocaine $178,560, Heroin $200,640, Methamphetamine $83,520 and Marijuana $19,440.

Additional costs include: loss of personal productivity, lower lifestyle, increased illness, DUI arrests, loss of work due to illness and jail time, increased insurance costs (car and health), loss of earned income, general money problems, and the cost of ending an addiction (multiple attempts are not uncommon).

I realize that many people in their early twenties think they are bulletproof and immortal. It's just not worth it no matter how "cool" it seems, at the time.

19. Poor choices – The choices you make over time have a "life cost" associated with them. They affect your life and your money.

> IT'S ALL ABOUT *YOUR* CHOICES: I once guest lectured at a college fraternity about the epidemic problem with underage drinking and drug use, and drunk driving. It was part of a talk on making smart choices in life. After my talk the president of the pledge class (who was under the drinking age) announced that he had to resign because he got a DUI the weekend before. Argh! That short-term choice to drink and drive will have a long-lasting negative impact. You always have to ask after the fact: Was it worth it? And the answer is always the same: No.

Other examples of poor choices include: buying things you can't afford or don't need because of addictions to buying and accumulating things, owning pets that you can't take care of, buying into business deals that you don't understand, poor job choices, poor friend or relationship choices, missing credit card payments and getting stuck with increased interest rates, not understanding the financial contracts you have signed, making uninformed stock purchases and then selling lower because of panic, and simple lack of good financial education about living below your means. I could go on...

I can't put an exact cost on all of these, though I'm sure some people may have tried. Needless to say, the costs can be to your personal health from stress and also to your financial health.

The point is: The difference between a healthy and happy life and one that isn't, is based on choices. Having trusted friends, mentors and financial advisors helps you make better choices. Everyone has to make an effort to become more financially savvy. You have to care more about your own personal finances than anyone else. You can't simply delegate this to someone because you are bored with it or don't want to "waste" your time thinking about it.

20. End of Life costs – No one can avoid dying. (Sorry, not a fun topic...not that a lot of the 20 topics in this chapter have been.) That's probably the last thing on your mind right now...at least I hope so! How we live can have a big impact on our health and how we pass on.

There are government entitlement programs that are there to help people today and as they age. These programs may not exist when you get older. I don't want to sound alarmist but I'm not sure they will exist for me either.

Here are some quick descriptions from Dictionary.com and Investopedia.com:

> **Social Security:** A program of old-age, unemployment, health, disability, and survivors insurance maintained by the U.S. federal government through compulsory payments by specific employer and employee groups.

> **Medicare:** A U.S. government program of hospitalization insurance and voluntary medical insurance for people

aged 65 and over and for certain disabled persons under 65. It is attached to Social Security and available regardless of income. Some parts of the program are paid by taxes and deductions and some parts are paid by out-of-pocket by participants.

Medicaid: A U.S. government program, financed by federal, state and local funds, of hospitalization and medical insurance for persons of all ages (including those who are older) within certain income limits. Medicaid is the nation's largest single source of long-term care funding.

According to DailyFinance.com (an AOL website), Dartmouth researchers found that during the last two years of life total Medicare spending ranges from an average of $53,432 (for patients who were treated at the Mayo Clinic in Minnesota) to $93,842 (for those who were treated at the UCLA Medical Center in Los Angeles). Either way that's a lot of money.

The above only tells part of the story though. According to the Society for Medical Decision Making, out-of-pocket medical expenditures incurred prior to the death of a spouse could deplete savings and impoverish the surviving spouse. They concluded that most elderly adults would recommend forgoing costly end of life treatments if it was going to deplete the couple's savings.

~

So there's some of what life can throw at you...and, where applicable, the costs associated with each. Sounds scary huh? It's not so scary if you are aware, and consciously doing the right thing and making smart choices. Just having all this laid out in front of you may give you a different perspective on life.

Can you think of any other life choices that might cost you a lot of money? If you can, research them on your own and find out what you are getting into...before you get into it. Be prepared for what life has waiting for you and live it to the fullest. In the end it's all about the quality of the choices you make.

Chapter 25

~

Why every marketer
wants a piece of your wallet

They want your money. All of it!

News Flash: As a new graduate you are a sitting duck for marketers who are eager to sell you stuff that you didn't know you needed - and probably don't need. Sorry to say this, but it is assumed that you are easily influenced into making purchase decisions at this point in your life. I think that you are smarter than that...but then again I'm not trying to sell you anything.

This should say it all: One of the first ads to appear on Facebook when it was only targeting .edu (college) sites was from a credit card company. (Source: *The Facebook Effect*, David Kirkpatrick, Simon & Schuster, 2010.)

Let's make the safe assumption that everyone will be trying to get their hands in your pockets and take your money. That's a little extreme sounding, but it's actually quite true...they are just more polite about it than I just was. Think critically before you open up your wallet to anyone.

Now that you're getting a new paycheck (or soon will be) you'll have a target on your back. Think big dollar signs surrounded by blinking neon arrows. Chances are that you don't have a lot of financial commitments yet, other than a credit card and student loans, so you theoretically have disposable income that marketers will do their best job of convincing you to part with. If you haven't created a budget for yourself or any sort of financial plan yet you are more vulnerable to the marketing pitches that say: "It's only $XX per month so why not go ahead and do it? You need it!" While you are basking in the glow of having just graduated and settling into first-job reality, know that you are an easy mark unless you protect yourself.

Have you ever noticed how an avalanche of marketing starts right around graduation time? If you haven't, you will. It's a lot like political ads around election time, and equally as annoying. Need a new car? Need a house? Need whole life insurance? Need a bunch of credit cards? Need to take a graduation trip? Need a set of non-stick cookware? Need a set of knives? Need a new cell phone with all the upgraded services...voice, data, Wi-Fi, 4G? Need HD cable with every channel and a DVR? Want to find your soul mate? Want to chat live with singles in your area? The list goes on and on. Unfortunately your money doesn't.

There are a few things that you do need to spend your money on and that will be covered in the pages ahead. You've been so good at living inexpensively while at college that a little money in your hands feels good...but don't let it slip away. Once it's gone you can't get it back. In 5-10 years you probably won't remember all those things that you "thought" you needed...but really didn't.

Chapter 26

~

What your first paycheck might look like

*You got your first paycheck
and you're throwing cash around.
What happened to all your money,
did you lose it on the ground?*

Let's say you scored that average "just out of college" annual paycheck of around $48,000. That's $4,000 a month in "gross" dollars. $4,000 is a lot of money, but don't be surprised when you don't see that entire number making its way into your checking account.

I'm going to warn you that this next section might be a little depressing. Sorry! But at least you will know this information now, and not when it's too late.

According to the paycheckcity.com paycheck calculator estimator tool, in 2011 your semi-monthly paycheck with no additional deductions, no extra withholding and filing single might look like the following three examples:

EXAMPLE 1: ALASKA, FLORIDA, NEVADA, NEW HAMPSHIRE, SOUTH DAKOTA, TENNESSEE, TEXAS, WASHINGTON & WYOMING

These states have no state individual income taxes. (New Hampshire & Tennessee tax dividend and interest income only.) This example is for Florida.

Semi-Monthly Gross Pay	$2,000.00
Federal Withholding	$330.77
Social Security	$84.00
Medicare	$29.00
Semi-Monthly Net Pay	$1,556.23
Annual Take-Home Pay	**$37,349.52**

EXAMPLE 2: CALIFORNIA

California has a state income tax & state disability income insurance. (Note: Other payroll taxes may exist depending on the city you live in or where your company is based.)

Semi-Monthly Gross Pay	$2,000.00
Federal Withholding	$330.77
Social Security	$84.00
Medicare	$29.00
California	$93.27
CA SDI	$24.00
Semi-Monthly Net Pay	$1,438.96
Annual Take-Home Pay	**$34,535.04**

EXAMPLE 3: NEW YORK

New York has a state income tax, state disability income insurance and New York City resident tax.

Semi-Monthly Gross Pay	$2,000.00
Federal Withholding	$330.77
Social Security	$84.00
Medicare	$29.00
New York	$103.35
NY SDI	$1.20
City Tax (Resident)	$61.31
Semi-Monthly Net Pay	$1,408.56
Annual Take-Home Pay	**$33,368.88**

That's quite a difference from the starting $48,000, right? Now that you know what's going to happen it won't be such a surprise.

To see what the tax picture is like in state you will be living in, use paycheckcity.com or type: *"salary paycheck calculator"* in your favorite search engine for more information.

Chapter 27

~

Before you do anything with your money: Have a financial plan

As noted earlier, your number one financial goal when you graduate and get your first job should, first and foremost, be to have a "financial plan." But what does that look like, exactly?

There are many "pieces" to your financial future and you get to them by taking a series of steps, which is also known as having a process. It's easy to know where you are going in your financial plan when you have a map in place.

A financial plan can put you on a path to financial freedom. I know, it sounds like a late night infomercial...sorry! You can rarely do everything in your financial plan all at once. Take your time and get it right. Your financial plan is all about setting priorities about how and when you will use your money.

Think of your financial plan like a process:

1. You need money coming in:
    = job / paycheck
2. To live you will need to spend money:
    a. You need to live somewhere:
        = rent + monthly rent
        related bills + insurance

b. You need to get around:
= transit pass or vehicle + insurance
c. You need to pay off your credit card debt monthly:
= credit card payment
d. You need to pay off student loans:
= loan repayment
3. To have a future you'll need to save money:
a. You need to build up cash reserves:
= Emergency Fund and then a future investment fund
b. You need to think about your financial future:
= investments + retirement + other financial goals
4. You want to live and enjoy your life

How do you get all that organized and make it happen? The next chapter shows you how to build a tactical plan to guide you.

Chapter 28

~

Creating your "must have" financial plan

Having money changes everything in your life.

Regardless of whether you are making more or less than $48,000 year, there are some important financial planning concepts that you'll need to consider.

They are:

1. Keeping your finances under control
2. Living within your means

3. Having no financial "surprises" that you can't handle
4. Planning for your long term financial and life goals
5. Having fun along the way

Here's how to think through your financial plan:

1. Define your overall money goals
   What are you saving/investing for and when will you need the money?
2. Set up an Emergency Fund – to cover unexpected expenses
   Once your Emergency Fund is "fully funded" you can start focusing on the rest of your money goals
3. Set a budget
   a. Monthly living expenses (rent, car + insurance, utilities, cell phone, etc.)
   b. Insurance
      i. Disability
      ii. Renters
      iii. Term Life
      iv. Health
   c. Monthly student loan re-payments
   d. Credit card debt repayment
   e. Food, Entertainment, Misc.
4. Use your credit card on a cash only basis and pay it off monthly
   Know your credit limit and your APR (Annual Percentage Rate) even if you plan on paying the card off monthly
5. Have an Investment Plan - Financial goals tied to life goals, appropriate asset allocations, etc.
6. Set up Dedicated Savings Accounts for vacation, newer car, holiday travel and gifts, etc.

Now let's start to break this all down:

A financial plan is the center of your money universe. Start by defining what you want the money you will be accumulating to do for you.

What are your money goals?

- Do you want to fund future education?
- Make investments to accomplish a life goal?
- Create a bigger cash safety blanket of a certain amount?
- Buy a house in the next few years?
- Start a business in a year?
- Get married and have kids in a certain time frame?

In what order of importance do all these things fall? And how much are the amounts associated with each one? When do you want to have these accomplished by? You can't really do anything more until you've figured out what your money goals are.

Take some time to list your top 3–5 money goals in the order of importance to you. Keep them in front of you in whatever way works best. Meeting those goals is what you'll want to focus your financial plan on.

How do you fund your financial plan?

Start with the basic concept of spending less than you make and putting away the rest. Let's call it a "rule" to make it more important to you. It's called "living below your means" and it's a concept that everyone seems to have heard about before but few people are able to grasp, much less accomplish. Those who do live within their means are always better off financially. You can usually spot them in a crowd; they're smiling and seem at ease.

124

How much you make really doesn't matter when it comes to living below your means...to a point. People at almost any income level can accomplish this, though it does require more creativity when you don't make much. As one recent graduate points out: "Spending less than you make is not something society teaches us. So you have to 'create' that habit."

Part of your financial plan includes an investment plan. You only want to execute on your investment plan *after* your Emergency Fund is full, and preferably after you've paid off your student loans and credit card bills. That doesn't mean that you can't be planning for it in the meantime. You'll have plenty of time to start making investments in the future. Resist the temptation to succumb to any investment "opportunities" until you are ready. There will always be some big opportunity that might derail you from sticking to your plan.

Chapter 29
~
Why you need a budget

Budget = Smart
No Budget = Clueless and Broke
Pick one.

It's simple, you need a budget so that you'll know you are living below your means. Yes, it's the dreaded "B" word to some people. Personally, I think budgets are beautiful things. Just like a GPS is a beautiful thing to have when you are lost.

Consider the "standard" budget checklist questions that ask: "What do you take in every month? What are your bills? And what's left over to save?" This thinking has been around for years. The fatal flaw with it is that "what's left over to invest" is always last in line. By the time you get there you've already found creative ways to spend almost everything you've made, if not more. It puts your priorities in the wrong order, so let's change that:

Instead of putting saving last, put it first.

"Off the Top" Savings – You'll see an immediate difference in your personal finances by making saving a top priority. You need to take funds "Off the Top" for your savings and then look at what's left to pay your bills. It will make you think twice about what you are spending money on. Set a percentage that works for you, the higher the better. You make the call. It's always a good idea to model these budgets on a spreadsheet. Financial modeling shouldn't be difficult. My personal rule is to always keep it simple. A sample budget template is shown in the next chapter.

Future Investments – Depending on your financial goals you will ultimately want to invest your money in multiple places. This is where a financial advisor can help you. Asset categories you should be thinking about would include: Index funds, individual stocks, an IRA or Roth IRA, real estate (or REITS - Real Estate Investment Trusts - they are a fund made up of real estate properties), bonds and cash. This is all *after* you've set up an Emergency Fund that is only available for big things like an unexpected major car repair, medical expenses, job loss expenses, etc.

Student Loan Re-Payment – If you have student loans to repay, you will want to create a line item for them and adjust your budget accordingly. If your student loans are large you may need to minimize your other expenses. Always minimize the Emergency Fund last.

Emergency Fund – As mentioned previously, an Emergency Fund should cover about 3-6 months of living expenses. Six months is preferable. An emergency is considered something catastrophic that you did not anticipate. That does not include: 20" chrome wheels, a gym membership or a yoga vacation.

The only exception I can think of is if you are secure in your job and you have a great investment opportunity presented to you. The same rule of "investing only what you can afford to lose" still applies. If you decide to trim your Emergency Fund from 6 months don't let it go to less than 3 months; and start replenishing it immediately. Balance all the risk factors and be cautious of the momentary excitement that's created around any supposedly "big" opportunity.

Credit Cards – As part of your financial plan you'll also need a credit card. One or two will do. Get a reasonable credit limit and interest rate, and find a card with the perks that you can use. Use the card only for items that you have the cash to pay for. Set aside an amount of cash that you will use to pay-off the card with each month.

Insurance & Benefits – Do you think that the company you are working for (or will be) has you completely covered with your benefits package? Think again. You might want to double-check that. It's hard for companies to offer a full suite of benefits these days with costs escalating as they are. You will also want to have some portability of your benefits even if you think you'll be staying put for a while. Portability means that you pay the policy premiums and the coverage moves with you wherever you go. You never know what can happen and it's always good to lock in lower premiums now.

There are four types of insurance that you'll want to have to protect yourself:

> **Disability Insurance** – According to finweb.com: "Disability insurance is one of the cheapest types of insurance coverage that you can purchase, comparatively speaking that is, and a young person can add future increase options to a disability insurance plans that will provide coverage for higher income limits as the young policy holder grows older. In fact, choosing a non-cancelable, guaranteed renewable disability insurance policy when

you're young is one of the smartest financial decisions a young person can make."

This would be a good "portable" policy to pay for on your own and take with you from company to company, throughout your career. A "graded premium" policy, which has lower premiums when you are younger, would cost around $30 a month.

Renters Insurance – Renter's insurance covers the contents of the place you are renting (i.e.: your personal stuff). What would it cost you to replace your things if they were stolen or lost in a fire? It may not seem like you have much but it all adds up and isn't something you could just write a check for if it was stolen. When you talk to your insurance company make sure your computer gear is covered...sometimes there are limits or additional policy coverage is required. It's inexpensive and if you have a roommate who happens to forget to lock the door or you do...you will be glad you had some insurance. This is another: "Ask me how I know" scenario.

Your company does not cover renters insurance. Typical cost for renters insurance is $125+ annually.

> FIRE! FIRE! FIRE! – UH-OH: While I was writing this book I heard television coverage of a fire at a rental home across town from me. It got big news coverage. The home burned down. While everyone was safe all the renter's belongings were destroyed. The news anchors pointed out that the renters did not have renter's insurance. I didn't know whether I should have felt sorry or embarrassed for them.

Term Life Insurance – Term life insurance is the best value for most people. Whole life policies are insurance plus forced savings plans that are very profitable for insurance companies. With the investment plan that you are modeling (and assuming you will stick with it) you will do better to buy term insurance and make your own investments according to your plan. That's assuming you actually make your own investments.

You should have term life insurance to cover your liabilities, take care of a spouse/partner/children and cover your funeral expenses. You may have some coverage from your employer as well...so make sure that you know what the size of the policy is. Check efinancial.com for more quote information.

This would also be a good portable policy to pay for on your own and take with you throughout your career. A term policy is extremely inexpensive when you are young. The premium for a $250,000 30-year term life policy on a 23-year-old male who doesn't smoke and is in very good health is around $20 a month. Well worth it.

Health Insurance – The company you work for may already cover a portion of your health insurance. With recent changes to health care more companies are eliminating co-pays and going to a shared-cost co-insurance structure plus an office visit fee ($25-35). You will be responsible for 20-30% of the medical bill that is negotiated by your health care provider.

Important Tip: This is why you need an Emergency Fund or better yet, a dedicated medical fund (in the form of a Health Savings Account – if applicable to you). Annual deductibles range from $1,000-$5,000. That's a lot of money if you have a medical emergency.

If your company covers your health care costs then divert this extra money into your Emergency Fund or student loan repayments. The sooner you have built your Emergency Fund and paid off your student loans the better off you will feel. That's a big part of your overall mental health too.

If your company doesn't offer health insurance you can buy it on your own. Premium rates run from $100-$215 a month in the Seattle area for a non-smoking male who is age 23. Go to: eHealthInsurance.com for more background information.

Always make sure that your insurance advisor knows all the various policies that your employer provides so they can make recommendations on what the best additional and overall coverage levels might be.

It's often cheaper to combine car, renters and other insurance policies together to get a better package price. Shop competitively and beware of low initial teaser rates that are increased after a period of time. It's also good to shop your insurance around every two years or so. Good sources for multiple lines of insurance include: StateFarm.com, Allstate.com, Geico.com, Farmers.com, and Progressive.com.

Pop Quiz: Do you have a will?

As long as we are on the topic of assets and insurance...the last thing you will probably be thinking about right now is a will, but you should have one, especially if you are married or getting married. It will be pretty simple at this point of your life because you will probably have already specified beneficiaries on all your insurance policies.

It's easy to get a form from a legal resource website on the Internet. Type: "legal wills online" into your favorite search engine for more information. The beneficiaries of a simple will are usually your family or spouse or some combination of those people. It won't be that difficult to create one.

Have you ever heard of a Directive Letter?

In addition to your will you might also want to have a document called a "directive letter." It will state how you want non-financial instruments like cars, keepsakes, etc. distributed after your death. You might be acquiring and/or selling a few things in your early years, so this easily changeable letter should suffice. You shouldn't change your will just because you bought a different car or a new sofa.

Make sure all the appropriate people have copies of the directive letter and will in a sealed and dated envelope. That way you will know which version is the most current.

Chapter 30

~

What your monthly budget might look like

Budgets are important tools for financial success, as long as you stick with them. Most people have no idea how to create one.

Here's a simple budget that has all the basics:

It assumes that gross salary of $4,000 a month and that you are living alone.

MONTHLY INCOME:

Take-home pay: $3,000.
Assumes $1500 bi-monthly.
After taxes and other deductions.
"Off the Top" savings (-15%)   <u><$450></u>

That $450 is diverted to your Emergency Fund and then ultimately to you savings/investment accounts.

Money available for expenses $2,550

MONTHLY EXPENSES:

Rent*	$750
Utilities *	$120
Food	$250
Transportation	$320
(Vehicle, Insurance, Fuel)	
Cell Phone	$100
Cable/Internet*	$100
Disability Insurance	$30
Renter's Insurance*	$15
Term Life Insurance	$20
Health Insurance	$150
Credit Card Payment	$200
Student Loans**	$280
Entertainment	$115
Giving Back***	$100

GRAND TOTAL $2,550

There's no way to know what everyone's budget might look like because of individual debt obligations. This budget is an example, but the budget line items should definitely be considered when building your own budget.

FOOTNOTES:

* Items that can be potentially split with a roommate.

**Assumes average student loan debt of $24,000 @ 6.9% in 2010 and paid-off over 10 years. Total interest paid will be just over $9,200. Type: "student loan calculator" in your favorite search engine for more information.

***A quick word about the "Giving Back" line item in the budget example above: In my book *The Frugal Millionaires* one thing that all the millionaires I interviewed had in common was that they donated money to charity. It seems unusual to think that you'd be doing that being just out of college, especially if you have some hefty debts, but giving back is a good habit to get into no matter how much you give. Every little bit helps. If you can't spare the money, then donate your time and expertise to a local charity that aligns with your values. We can never give back enough. Consider making a tribute to all the friends, family, teachers, mentors and other people who helped you get where you are today. People who give will tell you that the more you give the more you get back.

~

A NOTE ABOUT BEING OVERLY CHARITABLE: I've read about a couple in Seattle that was donating more to charities than to their retirement accounts. They were trying to save the world without thinking about the impact on their own finances and retirement. This thinking is crazy! They got carried away thinking they were doing the right thing. Good for them, but your personal finances come first. This is not a selfish thought, but rather a practical one. Help others whenever and however you can. If you do it in a smart way you can give more over longer periods of time.

What about automating your personal finances and budget?

Is creating a simple spreadsheet to track your budget not your thing? If you'd like to be more automated and keep track of your personal finances online from your laptop or smart phone (I think there is an app for that...!), you do have some robust options. Each site below does things a little bit differently so I'll let you explore them and see which one is right for you.

Consider these options:

- Mint.com (free and owned by Intuit, it's the one all the others compare themselves to)

- Learnvest.com (free to sign-up, targeted at women, features boot camps to get users "in-shape" financially)
- Buxfer.com (free)
- Budgetpulse.com (free)
- NetworthIQ.com (free)
- Budgettracker.com (free, or a small monthly fee for an ad-free version)
- Mvelopes.com (free trial, then monthly fee).

Use your favorite search engine to find current reviews of these products to see if they will fit your needs. They do require a little bit of set-up, but once it's done you will be in better control of your budget and personal finances. Many of the students I know rave about these sites.

Chapter 31

~

The X% savings factor

It's not what you make, it's what you keep, AND what you do with it.

You can't just save your way to great wealth...ultimately you will invest most of your money. Getting in the habit of putting away money so it can accumulate and grow is an ongoing theme of *First Job ~ First Paycheck*. Saving takes money out of your "spending" stream so you can put it to better use later. This is why taking money "Off the Top" is so important. Is this all starting to make sense now?

You've got to have your own seed money to start your investment career, just like a start-up needs seed money from an angel investor. In this case you are investing in your own financial future. That makes you your own angel, so pick your own "Off the Top" saving percentage: 5%-10%-15+%...the higher the better. When you save it first you'll never miss it. You will adjust your lifestyle accordingly. If you are also taking 5% "Off the Top" and sending it directly into a retirement account you are doing yourself an even bigger favor.

Most people have no major paycheck until their first job out of college. If you've learned to live on mac-and-cheese, rice, beans, corn, canned tuna and the occasional Red Bull (that stuff is not good for you!) you are in a perfect position to live below your means and start saving once you are making money. Now you can focus on accumulating savings and building your future. Yes, it takes focus and determination, and a few people actually are smart enough to do this. Be one of them.

Chapter 32

~

Before you invest in anything, please save...a lot

Save, Save, Save. Invest some of it. Repeat...

Your financial plan, like you, is a work in process...so first things first. There's a rule in investing that I mentioned earlier. It says: "Only invest what you can afford to lose." Right now, with your first job and your first paycheck, you can afford to lose absolutely nothing. Zero. Zip. Zilch. Nada. You are getting established financially so stick to your game plan.

After my college lectures I always have students who come up to me and ask "Where should I invest?" They typically attach a number to it...like $10,000. My immediate answer is: Do you have an Emergency Fund? If not then invest nowhere, right now anyway. Instead, "invest" that money in your Emergency Fund, even if the interest rates are ridiculously low.

Chances are good that once you get your first job you'll still have college bills to pay. If you don't then you'll be able to build that Emergency Fund even faster.

The hardest thing to do in this book is learning how to save... and save a lot. Quite frankly, we Americans are *really bad* at saving. We've only saved because we were scared to spend or invest during the Great Recession. Fear is not a great motivator to get you excited about doing anything.

I've openly admitted that saving is boring. That is until you've accumulated a bunch of money and you feel more confident about your financial future. Then it's a whole different game. Unfortunately we are in a consumer economy and that is why so many people are broke, but they have nice stuff...argh! Let me save you years of ulcers and stress by getting you into the correct habit of saving at an early age.

Once you start to build up resources it will hit you that you have more power over your personal finances and more freedom to do the things financially that you want to do. Sure, everyone else around you might be partying all the time and spending all of their newly earned money like reality TV or rock stars. But that's just it they're *spending* it, not *growing* it.

I'm willing to go out on a limb here and say that the more money you save the less inclined you will be to want to waste it over time. Once you see the "zeros" adding up in your savings account the less likely you will want to part with it on silly things, like your friends might be doing. You will want to find interesting ways to make your money work smarter for you. Those who spend money as fast as they make it (or worse - faster!) will never have the feeling of financial well-being that you will.

Savings accounts are about safety and that's about all they offer you. They won't pay big interest...but that's not the point right now. Savings accounts are the initial part of an overall financial plan. They help you get into a habit of putting money in a place so that it can work harder for you later. If you create the right habits early enough then you are setting yourself up for financial greatness.

Set up a savings account and label it "Emergency Fund" (are you getting tired of hearing this yet?) Once you have 3-6 months of expenses saved up, then and only then, should you start testing the investment waters, and that's only with a strong investment plan in place, of course.

Chapter 33

~

What your investment plan might look like

Live in the moment.
Invest for the future.

An investment plan creates places to put your money and help it grow. It helps you create the funds that help you meet your financial goals.

The components of a financial plan are pretty straightforward. It's making the allocations to those components that can be challenging for some and elementary for others.

The basic components of your "starter" investment plan look like this:

- **Emergency Fund**

- **Savings Account** - A holding pen for future
    investment funds

- **401(k)** - I put this here because your employer may
    have a matching program and contributions
    can be deducted automatically from your
    paycheck. That's a great deal for you and it's
    always a good idea to take advantage of free
    money.

You must have the above established before jumping into
these:

- **Investments**
    - Index Funds (they track the general
        markets)
    - Individual Stocks (good if you have deep
        knowledge of companies and
        understand a market segment)
    - International Funds (the world is a global
        economy now)
    - Bonds (generally slow and steady, better
        interest than a savings account, often
        tax free)
    - Investment grade real estate / REITs

- **Voluntary Retirement Accounts**
    - IRA (taxed when you start drawing on it)
    - Roth IRA (created with after tax dollars so
        you are not taxed when withdrawing
        at retirement age)

- **Special Savings Accounts**
    - Very goal specific: education, vacation,
        marriage, etc.

- **Buying a house**

What about Mutual Funds?

I don't mention mutual funds under "Investments" because I am not a big fan of them. I like "true" Index Funds better. Mutual fund managers rarely outperform the market indexes and you pay them big fees to try. Any mutual fund that underperforms the market does not add value to your financial plan.

Unfortunately, 401(k) plans typically have a large mutual fund component to them. Your mutual funds choices are usually controlled by the financial institution that administers your 401(k). If you are given a choice of "Index Funds" take them (more on those later). If you are stuck with mutual funds then pick wisely. Also ask what kind of fees you are paying. Later in life, you can move your 401(k) accounts into an IRA account. Then you will be able to self-direct your asset choices and allocations to the funds you choose.

Isn't a home an investment?

I also don't mention a home under "Investments" above. I've said this before, but your home isn't a "liquid" investment. That means it can't be quickly turned into cash to take advantage of new market opportunities. (Also see page 166.) Unless you have a Home Equity Line of credit, which really can't happen until you've built up a lot of equity in your home.

Chapter 34

~

Making your budget fit your salary

If I only made more money, I'd be rich. (= False)
If only I spent less money, I'd be rich. (= True)

Even some people who make a lot of money have a problem with making their budget fit their salary.

A PAINFUL REAL LIFE CASE STUDY: I had a good friend who was making $200,000 a year and he told me that he was having trouble making ends meet. He was in the process of getting a divorce and his life was turned upside down. He was draining his retirement account to make up the difference between his $200,000 salary and his actual expenses. I could have just cried for the guy...not because he was getting a divorce (OK, that too), but more because he was in such a financial mess even though he was making that kind of money. As it turns out, that's pretty common. A scary thought.

He asked me to help him find a better job...maybe one that was paying $250,000-$300,000 a year. Oh, and this was during the Great Recession! The first thing I asked him was if he had a budget. "Oh yes," he said, and he and his soon to be ex-wife had gone over it with a microscope to save money. They had "cut expenses to the bone." There was nothing left to trim. Um, OK. Let me ask you, the reader: Do you find it hard to believe on a $200,000 a year income that you can't make ends meet? I did, but it happens every day.

I asked him what his two biggest expenses were. One was the $5,000+ mortgage on his $900,000 house. The other was private school for his two very young kids... and that was about $4,000 a month. "OK," I said, "You don't need to make more money...that's everyone's excuse! You need to live within your means and stop fooling yourself about your lifestyle."

Then we got deep into it. I asked him: "Why don't you downsize the house and put the kids in a good public school for a few years? You are killing yourself financially and depleting your retirement too." The response was that he and his soon to be ex-wife felt the kids *needed* a private school upbringing just like they had and they *needed* to grow up in a house with a yard. Yep, and I *need* a Ferrari and a 100' motor yacht. Right? R-i-ight. No.

I told him that I understood how this predicament was created, but did he realize that being completely broke and living in that big house and sending his kids to an expensive private school made no financial sense at all? His kids would be just fine in public school and living in a smaller house. The kids were young and the only people all this stuff mattered to were the parents. Their pride was at stake...make that *ego* instead. They were the ones who couldn't face reality, not their kids.

He ultimately sold the house, *and* got a higher paying job when the economy got better. That sounded like a reasonable compromise to me. Progress comes in small steps. The lesson learned? Never, ever, should you compromise your retirement and investments when you have other options.

~

Let's say you've gone through the budget process and your budget doesn't seem to fit your salary, just like my friend above (though not at the same $$$$ level!). Here are some things you can do to make it work:

1. **Get a roommate.** You are probably already used to this from your recent college days...and in this economy maybe living by yourself isn't in the cards just yet. Having a roommate can cut your costs in half on just about everything, plus you have someone to talk to and you might be able to live in a little nicer place for less money. The alternative is that you can move home.

2. **Look at your recurring monthly expenses.** At this point in your life all your bills are recurring expenses and they can kill your budget. See what you really need compared to what you really want. This requires some critical thinking. Do you really need the phone plan with all the perks? The same goes with cable. Do you need a health club membership when there are so many less expensive ways to get a work out? Do you need to spend cash whenever you go out when there are plenty of free or inexpensive things you can do that make life no less interesting? One graduate is fond of checking out the local city resource websites to find free things to do. Tapping into this kind of thinking will make you and your budget happier.

3. **Look at your annual cost structure.** You can review your insurance and raise deductibles if you have been accident free. But be aware that having to pay a few good deductible hits can cost you a lot of money. If you are accident prone stick with the lower deductibles.

You can also raise/lower the thermostat to lower your electrical bills, reduce your cell phone minutes, use coupons (for things you *really* need), and look at your transportation costs to see if there is a more efficient way: like public transportation, ride-sharing, car-sharing, bicycling or buying a lower priced/more efficient vehicle.

Chapter 35

~

But I want cool stuff...now

Living beyond your means makes you a poseur.

In my book *The Frugal Millionaires* the average time that the people I interviewed had been millionaires was nine years. One of the questions I asked them for my research was "What is your most prized possession and how long have you had it?"

I didn't really care what kind of stuff they had (though one millionaire's prized possession was a 15-year-old Saab Convertible...his kids loved it! Go figure...). I was more interested in how long they had owned their prized possession compared to how long they had been millionaires. The answer was seven years and it proved to be an important point.

If the millionaires had been so for nine years, but only had their prized possessions for seven years, that means they had waited until they were already millionaires to acquire these possessions. One secret of their success was that they didn't take money out of their potential income stream before they became wealthy. They waited until later to reward themselves.

When I got my first job after college I noticed a lot of my peers had gone out and leased nice German cars and bought more house than it seemed they would ever need, or could afford at the time. Then they started taking super expensive vacations and eating out a lot. They were living a lifestyle that their salaries couldn't support. Why? Because that's how they were brought up – and that's a key point that I've been trying to make throughout the book: The *often-repeated myths* about money don't work any longer. In the past most people thought that the money would never stop flowing and there would always be *more* of it. How many of us today still don't know that the flow of money can come to a screeching halt at any time?

It's not just buying the big ticket items that can make you broke; you also have to maintain them, possibly pay monthly service fees on them, and you also have to consider the lost opportunity cost of spending money that could be invested and double or triple in value (or more) over your lifetime. Constant, impulsive splurges can also do you in. Do you really need that first job ~ first paycheck

new next generation iPad or iPod when the one you have now is just fine? How about those fancy designer sunglasses that will soon be out of style? The list goes on and on, but it all adds up. Recalibrate how you splurge. Reward yourself by keeping your money rather than spending it. This is a key concept. Why? Because the more money you spend on stuff earlier in your life the less you have over the rest of your life.

MODERN DAY ARCHEOLOGY: Here's one way to convince yourself that all your "got to have" impulse purchases might be a bad idea. Get a moving box and put all the stuff in it that you "just had to have" over the last year. Then consider sifting though it all like a modern day archeological dig. Look at all those things you just had to have and decide if you really, really needed them. I'll bet you didn't.

Chapter 36

~

The value of compounding when you are young

You are at the perfect age to take advantage of compounding right now. It is a "savings account" concept but it applies to other investment areas as well; and is simply money growing over time at a certain interest rate.

- If you start with $1,000 today (let's say you're 22) and it grows 6% annually it will be worth $12,250 by the time you retire at 65.

- If you start with $10,000 today that can become $122,500 by the time you retire at 65.

144

- If you put away $100 a month from age 22 until you retire that amount will be: $256,056 by the time you retire at 65.

I'm sure you get the idea, and like I've said: An idea is nothing until someone does something with it.

If you want to play with different savings scenarios type: *"savings calculator"* into your favorite search engine. I used the bankrate.com calculator tool.

The *well-memorized myth* for this type of example was always using 10% for the assumed annual investment growth. That might have been realistic before the Great Recession of 2008-2010 but today, not so much. That's why I use 6% instead.

If you save nothing, you'll have nothing.

Don't "hope" that your parents will leave you anything or that you'll win the lottery or that your ship will come in, etc. Smart people don't assume those things will happen, only the naïve do.

When you invest money in a good stock or index fund it also compounds like a savings account, but without the guarantees and safety. "Compounding" isn't generally the term that's used. It's usually called Return On Investment or ROI.

When you invest in a start-up that becomes successful (not recommended at your age, unless you are the start-up or working for one) your investment return is often referred to as a "multiple" return. If you invested $10,000 in a start-up and you made $100,000, your investment would yield a 10X return or a "multiple" of 10 times your initial investment.

These are all words for the same thing: How your money grows without you touching it.

The longer you invest your money the longer it has to grow. That's the real concept here. If you don't start early it's hard to make it up towards the end. It's also very stressful trying to play catch-up in your later years with your investment portfolio.

Here's an example that's often used to show how compounding works. It's unrealistic (because the amount doubles every day) but it proves a point. So, let's say that you take a penny and double it every day for 31 days. How much would you have at the end?

Day 1 = $.01
Day 2 = $.02
Day 3 = $.04

...fast forward...

Day 29 = $2,684,354.60
Day 30 = $5,368,709.20
Day 31 = $10,737,418.40.

If this seems unbelievable set up your own spreadsheet and see what happens.

Notice the difference a few days towards the end make. This proves that if you don't start investing early and then keep your hands off the investment right until you need it you won't get those extra days of compounding (or years of compounding, in the real world). As you can see above, the difference can be huge.

The real point is, if you put your money in a smart place it will grow without a lot of effort on your part. That's what you want, right? If you're going to be working hard your money should be too. In fact, over time your money should be working harder than you. That can't happen unless you put it away as early as possible.

You don't get wealthy just by saving however, that's just the first part of the equation. You have to save before you can invest. It looks pretty grim to see a savings account pay around 1%

interest (or a lot less!) these days, but it's really only a safe holding-pen for your future investments. Use it in that way.

Your twenties and thirties should be your super-smart financial years. Save and invest as much as you can and still enjoy your life. You'll be in a better position to enjoy your life more fully from start to finish knowing that you will be financially secure.

Unfortunately, we don't know if a lot of the government related financial support (Medicare, Social Security, etc.) will actually exist in the same form over the next 50-60-70 years. Better to assume that it won't exist and then reap any benefits as a bonus if they ultimately are there. Smart people take it upon themselves to manage all aspects of their personal finances. They don't just hope that it will magically be taken care of.

Chapter 37

~

Think you can't make money in the stock market during a recession?

Be cautious when others are investing.
Invest when others are being cautious.
When in doubt, use the history of
the stock markets as your guide.

During the Great Recession I read plenty of articles about Gen X'ers and Millennials (like you) being timid about investing money. They weren't into investing or trusting the financial system. All were valid thoughts. I've also read numerous articles about how recessions create great investment opportunities for those who are paying attention.

Many older investors, who had money in the market, lost it. Some of them were your parents or relatives. Those losses were only temporarily for many unless they bailed out of the stock market completely, which is historically a bad idea. Trying to "time" going in or out of the markets rarely works, and for every seller in the market there's someone else who is a buyer. It takes buyers and sellers to make a market. When markets are falling, what do the buyers know that the sellers don't? They know financial history.

Some of the losses people took during the Great Recession were their own fault. They were self-inflicted. They bought homes they had no place buying, and over-leveraged themselves to do it. They made investments with money they couldn't afford to lose. Even back in the early 2000's people were doing stupid things like leveraging their home equity lines of credit to buy Internet stocks – or buying it on margin. When the Internet bubble burst in 2000-2001 the stock market took a beating, and so did many investors. Sadly, a lot of honest people got caught in the crossfire along the way. When markets go down they don't give extra credit to the good investors over the bad ones. The bad experiences that people around you have had most likely tainted your trust in the stock market or investing in general. You'd probably rather shove money under your mattress these days.

What I'm about to tell you about investing in a recession may come in handy when the next recession hits...and it will. History has proven the points I'm about to make, over and over again.

I personally witnessed people make money in the last few mini-recessions over the last 20 years and during the Great Recession in 2008. And I've been one of them. While I don't offer investment advice I can give examples on how being a good student of financial history has worked well.

The entrepreneurial spirit of America exists today whether it's being a smart investor putting money in start-up or existing companies or starting a new company on your own. Both strategies can make money. When you have money that you can afford to invest consider the results of an experiment that I conducted during the Great Recession. Your results can and will vary.

THE EXPERIMENT

In early 2008 the stock market was humming along. The S&P 500 was flirting with the 1,500 mark again as it had done in the middle of 2007 and before. But by mid-2008 the S&P 500 was starting to falter. During the first two weeks of October 2008 it took a huge triple-digit drop. That was right when I launched my second book, *The Frugal Millionaires* - good timing for marketing purposes, right?

Unfortunately, people were starting to panic. On October 10th 2008 the S&P dropped below 900 and over 11 billion shares traded hands. That 40% drop from *over* 1500 to *under* 900 had taken just 10 months. Something was wrong...it's easy to look back now and see that.

Not once during the Great Recession did I sell any stocks. I simply looked at the history of the stock market to tell me that everything would be OK over time. I didn't listen to the mainstream media telling me that the sky was falling, but a lot of other people did. Do you know any of them? I was investing for the long term so a 2-4 year blip wasn't going to hurt me. Those that were using the stock market like savings and checking accounts weren't so lucky. They got killed. They weren't thinking. It was financial Darwinism at work.

Taking a calculated leap...

During October of 2008 I came up with an opportunistic investment plan. Starting November 3rd, 2008 and every Monday afterwards for twenty weeks I instructed my financial advisor to begin investing an equal amount of a portion of my cash holdings. I made no attempt to time the market. In fact the market continued to go down *after* I started investing. Did I panic? No. I saw it as even more of an opportunity.

The only way I was able to pull off this experiment was because I had a savings account with cash in it. If you are "liquid" during tough times you can make smart investment moves when others can't. This is why saving money is so important.

I started this investing experiment after doing a fair amount of historical research and listening to what was going on in the market. Then it was time to get on with it – there is money to be made. The amount I invested didn't matter. It could have been $25 or $25,000 each week...you know, whatever you can afford to lose. Right? The fact was that I didn't sit back and just stare at the market – I did something.

I invested weekly to help manage risk of trying to time the market by putting everything in all at once. The concept is called "dollar cost averaging." We'll see how that played out ahead. It's not some secret formula that only certain financial advisors have access to. It's pretty basic stuff and nothing that was super technical. Essentially, you take an equal amount of cash and invest it in certain time intervals over a set time frame. Your 401(k) works in a similar way because you contribute to it with each paycheck you get.

So what did I invest in? It was actually quite simple. Trust me on this one! I chose a *market weight index fund* that mirrored the S&P 500. If you aren't familiar with them, *market weight index funds* buy a number of shares in all the companies that make up a certain index like the S&P 500 or Russell 2000, etc. The investment is based on the proportional value of each company in the index to the overall Index. These types of index funds are the most accurate representation of a market that is available. Index funds aren't at all complicated. You are buying a piece of a major stock index and not individual stocks. A more complete explanation of Index Funds is offered in the Appendix.

*Scared and/or uninformed investors
won't make any money in a down market.*

How did my investment experiment work out?

From November 3rd, 2008 through the end of October 2010 (about 2 years) my S&P 500 Index Fund investment returned 41.7%. Not bad! It outperformed the S&P 500 over that same time frame. That was in what was admittedly one of the worst economic environments that we have ever experienced.

If I had invested the entire amount I had allocated over the 20 weeks all in one day as a "lump sum" (on November 3rd, 2008) my investment would have "only" returned 28.1% over the 2 years. That's because over those 20 weeks, while I was dollar cost averaging, the market continued to move up and down. On some Mondays the S&P 500 had gone down in value but my weekly investment amount stayed the same. That meant that I was able to buy more shares at a lower price for the same amount of money for a period of time. No matter which return you consider a 28.1% or 41.7% cumulative return isn't bad. Especially during a recession!

On the other hand...

If I had been paying more attention to Apple (APPL) as a stand-alone stock I would have noticed that despite being in a down economy Apple was bucking the trend by creating "must have" products. Oh, and everyone was buying them. Using the same date parameters as above, Apple stock was trading at $106.96 on November 3rd, 2008. It seemed to be in the stratosphere already but Apple was just getting started with all its new product launches. Two years later it was trading at $316.87 (pre stock split). That's a 296% cumulative growth rate and a fantastic return. (As it turns out, I had plenty of Apple stock in my S&P 500 Index Fund.)

Or, how about this...

If I had been savvy enough to look more deeply at individual stocks that had "big opportunity" written all over them I might have done even better. While I don't suggest this strategy to new investors, it does work for those who are long-time "students" of the stock market and the business world in general. They also have the time to do the research.

My father is a great example of that. He has driven Ford products for years and believes they are of good quality. Back in 2008 he knew Ford had recently hired Alan Mulally away from Boeing (in 2006) to be their new President and CEO. He also knew that Ford was taking no bailout money from the government. So he invested in Ford stock because he believed they were the best investment of the US automakers and he supports America. He actually bought Ford stock three times during the Great Recession.

If he had invested in Ford stock that same day I invested in the S&P 500 Index Fund he would have paid $2.13 a share. (He invested a bit later.) If he held on to it (which he did) and checked the stock price two years later when I checked the S&P 500 Index Fund price Ford would have been trading at $16.06 a share. That's a 754% cumulative growth rate. And just as a reminder...that's during a recession. That's a crazy great return! It should be no surprise to you that my father was a history major in his college years...I guess those degrees can pay off!

~

None of the above three examples were a sure thing, although the S&P 500 rebound was extremely predictable based on historical markers. That's why you have to pay attention to history to be a smart investor in the stock market.

Patient investors who do their homework can make money even in down markets. You just have to tune out all the negative news and stay focused. I will add that just because a market is down doesn't mean that you can just randomly invest in it and make money. You have to think about what you are doing.

That's how financial advisors can help you, but they aren't 100% right all of the time either.

~

To close this chapter here are some observations about investing during the Great Recession:

If you had stayed in the stock market when it starting crashing in 2008 you would almost be back to where you were initially by 2011. It's been a rough few years for almost every investor. That's why so many professional investors, like Warren Buffett, take the long-term view when investing. They don't use the stock market like an ATM machine.

If you sold stock or funds in 2008 when everyone else was selling you'd have taken a huge loss. The herd mentality back then was: Sell! Sell! Sell! It was panic time. Smart investors didn't panic they just stayed on course. Trying to time when to come back into a market is as difficult as deciding when to bail on it since you always leave money sitting on the table. Very few can pull it off and those that do are very lucky. The odds are against you. The only time you really want to exit a market is before you need the funds to meet one of your personal financial goals. If you are "in" for the long term your stress levels should be very low when you see day-to-day volatility.

Chapter 38

~

What if you do decide to buy a house right out of college?

For most people a house is the most expensive thing they will buy in their entire lifetime. As noted in Chapter 23, nearly 17%

of the students I polled expressed interest in buying a home as their #1 financial goal after graduating. It was the #2 response after getting a job. Is buying a house right out of college really a good idea?

Many people your age are renting today while they are getting their lives "figured out." One thing they have seen over the last few years is that when your home is the biggest asset you have, your net worth can be turned upside down and become hugely negative in a very short period of time.

In business school you are taught the concept of diversifying your investments to minimize your risks. So for all the people that rushed out and bought a house when they were young and held it...well, they got hit pretty bad in the Great Recession. They didn't follow the Golden Rule of Investing: Diversify. Don't let that bad history repeat itself with you. Learn from the mistakes of others, and don't repeat them.

If I haven't convinced you to wait on buying that house then here are some things to consider:

You might ask me: Aren't housing prices and mortgage rates are at their lowest ever...right now? Then I'd ask you: Can you afford it right now and is this part of your overall financial plan?

The answers depend on a lot of variables. If you have your personal finances in order maybe you should consider it. But it would be under a different set of rules than what you would have had to play by just a few years ago. Buying a house must fit within your financial plan and budget, it can't restrict you from meeting your other personal and financial goals, and you must continue to pay all your other bills and not feel stressed out about it.

You will most likely continue to benefit from the housing fallout over the next decade by being able to take advantage of lower housing prices depending on where you live. Why? Because there is plenty of supply at the moment...and more on the way as foreclosures make their way through the clogged financial and real estate systems. But some people might just spin that to mean that they can buy that formerly $500K home for $300K even though it's still $100K more than they should be spending. The motivation might be that house prices could go back up to pre-crash levels. Don't fall into that trap.

In Warren Buffett's 2011 letter "To the Shareholders of Berkshire Hathaway, Inc." he notes:

> *"...a house can be a nightmare*
> *if the buyer's eyes are bigger than his wallet and if a lender*
> *– often protected by a government guarantee –*
> *facilitates his fantasy.*
> *Our country's social goal should not be*
> *to put families into the houses of their dreams,*
> *but rather to put them in a house they can afford."*

For those of you who haven't heard of Warren Buffett, he is one of the world's wealthiest men and clearly one of it's smartest investors.

Now, here are some basic rules for investing in a home:

1. Never buy more home (in size and price) than you really need and don't look at what a house was once worth...only look at today's market comps and growth projections.

2. Don't think "prices will come back...soon." In my humble opinion, it will be years before homes grow their way back to pre-Great Recession prices, if ever. The only way it will happen is through very incremental appreciation gains over long periods of time, just like it used to be. In many markets home prices are still adjusting, albeit in much smaller increments than previously experienced.

3. For an investment in a house to be "smart" it needs to fit into your time frame and your finances.

4. Interest rates will start going up again at some point, but an interest rate alone shouldn't dictate your decision to buy a house. The real decision comes when you have enough of a down payment, great credit, some stability in your life, and knowing that you'll be in one place for a while.

~

Buying a home means that you are stuck with it until you can sell it. If your twenties are anything like mine were, you don't need to be tied down to one geographical area just because you subscribe to that *often-repeated myth* of wanting to own a home. Flexibility equals opportunity, and we all know how you Millennials love your flexibility. Sometimes a stronger sense of security can come from having money in the bank and the flexibility to do what you want.

When you are ready to settle down you'll probably know it. It's not just about doing what everyone else ahead of you in life has done or is telling you to do. Maybe misery does love company? They don't always get it right. The rules have changed and you get to benefit from them, but only when you acknowledge that the rules have changed. See what the real world is about before you get too settled. View it as an adventure and not a one-way trip into the scary unknown.

> REAL LIFE IDEA: The recent graduate, now an entrepreneur, who I mentioned in the two other "Real Life Idea" segments came up with an interesting solution to the dilemma of buying a home when you are young. His then girlfriend (now wife) and he decided they were ready to settle down and figured out that they could actually pay significantly less than what they were paying for rent and buy a place...while still retaining a lot of flexibility.

How did they do it? They bought a duplex and rented out the other side. It is both a real estate investment and a home. Smart. The "rent" from one side covers almost 75% of their total mortgage payment. When they are ready to get a bigger place they can turn their side of the duplex into another rental unit and immediately create positive cash flow.

It works for them. They found a way to live less expensively and create more cash flow. But being a landlord, especially when your tenant is living right next door, is not for everyone. As is true with every investment you make, the timing must be right, good finances should be in place, and some significant life choices need to be agreed to...in advance.

I spoke to a "mortgage specialist" to get you info on getting a mortgage at your age.

Note that your typical mortgage specialist gets paid when they sell you a mortgage. The bigger the mortgage, or the lower the down payment, the more they make. So they are going to try and get you into the biggest mortgage they realistically can... though maybe not as aggressively as in the past few years. They have a vested interest in convincing you that buying a home is one of the smartest investments you can make. The real estate agents will back them up on that. The truth is that the smartest investment you can make is the one that fits best into your financial plan. The fact that you also get a place to call "your home" is a nice emotional benefit.

If you are going to take the real estate plunge at some point, (pun semi-intended, in a bad economy anyway) you will need to know what you are doing. Do your homework (...have you heard that before?).

When it comes to mortgages there are a few things you need to know:

157

1. You need decent credit (OK, that's obvious). Minimum FICO score is 640-660 depending on the lender, although 620 is often doable but you will pay dearly for it. You really need to get your credit score over 760 to get the best interest rates.

2. You must have a job and a paycheck (W-2 or 1099-MISC). The days of no-proof-of-employment-required loans (aka: faking your income) are long gone. Thankfully.

3. The credit requirements are that you have three "trade lines" (lines of credit) with a 12-month clean credit history, and all three of your credit scores. Trade lines could include: a student or car loan, and a credit card.

4. Minimum down payment for an FHA loan is 3.5%. For a conventional loan it's 5%. If you are military and use the GI Bill after college you will most likely qualify for zero down.

> THOUGHTS ON DOWN PAYMENTS: A 3.5-5.0% down payment doesn't sound like much but it can be a lot of money depending on where you live. You should never compromise your financial plan to get into a mortgage until you are ready.

> Personally, I'd want to put down more than 5% to lower my payment and interest charges. I'd also want to be sure that my house value wasn't going to keep going down. And, I hate paying interest to banks. Yes, hate is a strong word, but it truly applies here.

> If you are struggling to save for a down payment you should think about just how ready you are to start making big house payments every month for the next 360 months = 30 years! That doesn't include any re-financing along the way, which starts the "30-year" clock all over again. That is unless you refinance to a 15-year mortgage. That would be doubtful because most people refinance to lower their monthly payment.

As I've mentioned previously, if you aren't in the habit of saving up money to buy something be cautious about accepting money from your family for a down payment. It may seem like a nice gesture but it could be a quick way to becoming house poor. If you aren't in command of your personal finances, don't get help to put yourself into debt buying the most expensive thing you will ever own.

5. 15 or 30-year fixed rate mortgages are the ONLY way to go, or shorter if you can possibly do that. The lower and longer the payment the more interest you will likely be paying.

Don't let anyone talk you into an adjustable rate mortgage or an interest-only loan. They are a lot like car leases that profess to "put you into something more than you normally could afford."

Chapter 39

~

6 ways millionaires think differently about money:

2% of the population are millionaires.
What do they know that you don't ?

In my book *The Frugal Millionaires* I asked 70 millionaires for their secrets on how to be smarter with money. I analyzed how they think differently about money than the other 98% of the population. Below is some of their thinking. The sooner you start to use them the better off you will be financially.

Before you say to yourself: "Of course those people can do those things...they're millionaires!" - think again. They have always thought this way. That, in large part, is why they are millionaires today. If you start these habits early enough in life you too could have similar results.

1. They make living below their means painless – They can buy a lot more of everything, but they choose not to play that game. They don't feel that they are making any sacrifices to live this way because they are not over-consumers like the rest of the population. They take deep pride in not wanting what everyone else thinks they absolutely need.

2. They make delayed gratification easy – They can effectively block the "impulsiveness" gene in their bodies so that they don't ever feel they "need something right now" – unless it is emergency medical care. Immediacy usually costs you more money. Do you always want the latest thing or want something right now? You'll pay more for the privilege. Timing is everything. They also won't over-leverage themselves on loans to get something, ever. They can wait to acquire things, if they acquire them at all.

3. They minimize their sense of self-entitlement – They don't say: "I want it, therefore I deserve it! Waah, Waah, Waah!" They will reward themselves when the time is right, and those rewards can be big, but they won't do it at the expense of their long-term financial goals. They keep in check the basic human nature of wanting to acquire more stuff just to show off to others. Remember, these are *frugal* millionaires...not the self-impressed conspicuously consuming D-Bags you see all over the media.

4. They are resourceful in getting what they want – Once they do decide they really need something they figure out the smartest and least costly way of getting it. They think and plan long before they act. This might take a little more of their time, but it is well worth it. They realize their time is more valuable than money but they don't put excessive convenience ahead of value received. In other words, they won't overpay like others will.

5. They don't like wasting anything, especially money – Just because they have money doesn't mean that they have to spend it excessively. They aren't here to impress others, they are here to enjoy life and help others. This is core to their thinking. If they don't waste their money then they also won't waste water, fuel, time, food and other resources. It's all interconnected for them.

6. They are OK with spending money, depending on what they are buying – They don't mind spending money as long as that means they are *investing* it in something. And, it's not always about financial investments. It could mean investing in people, or charities, or things; with the goal of creating a certain outcome that makes the world a better place. It's not *that* they spend, but rather *how* they spend.

Have you ever thought about money this way? Has what you just read changed the way that you might think about money in the future? If you don't have the kind of money mindset that you just read about it will be that much more difficult to achieve financial success.

Chapter 40

~

The top 7 frugal millionaire
money-making & money-saving tips:

*The less money you waste in life
the more you have
to spend on what's important to you.*

In *The Frugal Millionaires* I created a "model" frugal millionaire by laying out a set of best practices that millionaires have used to create and maintain wealth. Here are some of their tips that are most appropriate to your current situation:

161

TIP 1. Have a financial plan and an advisor – Frugal millionaires have financial advisors and so should you. As mentioned earlier, one of the main reasons I asked those 650 college students "what their number one financial goal was"... to see if they were thinking about a "plan." Advisors can help you create that plan, which becomes your investment road map. These maps can help you save a lot of money and make a lot of money.

Find an advisor that you can pay a small one-time fee to so they can set you up with a plan to follow. Seek out a great advisor through successful people and mentors that you trust. Word of mouth is key here.

If the advisor you choose offers competitive financial or insurance products then consider them, but you are not bound to buy anything from them. If your potential advisor tells you they offer "free" advising, insist on paying them a reasonable fee so that you won't feel obligated to buy anything.

A great advisor will tell you how much you should be allocating to various parts of your financial plan throughout stages in your life. Think in terms of life milestones...as in: age 25, 30, 35, 40, 45, 50 etc. But avoid the mutual funds that are tailored to age milestones.

You should also read books on this topic to help make you conversant about money before you meet with a financial advisor. (See the Recommended Reading List in the back of the book.) You are more involved in this process and have a greater vested interest in you than anyone else does.

Most frugal millionaires keep their investing simple and inexpensive because it really doesn't need to be that complicated. They balance their investments with retirement vehicles like a 401(k) (from their company), and a personal IRA and/or a Roth IRA. They also invest in bonds to balance their risk. They only accept more risky investments based on their risk tolerance.

The general rule of investing is that you can assume more risk the younger you are, so that means more Index Funds and/ or individual stocks. Your investment in bonds is minimal (if any) when you are young, but will increase as you get older and need that money to be secure for retirement. A great financial advisor will lay all this out for you – after listening to all your goals.

TIP 2. Take advantage of the stock market via low cost Index Funds – When you are ready, one way to invest in the stock market is to use Index Funds. They are a favorite of frugal millionaires. Index Funds were created so an investor has access to buying the returns of a general market. These types of funds track the major market indexes like the S&P 500, Wilshire 5000, Russell 2000, and EAFE (international stocks) etc., and they are easy to follow. The big advantage is that they have extremely low management fees.

The top companies offering Index Funds are: fidelity.com, schwab.com, and vanguard.com. There are others, but start with these. For more information type: *"lowest cost index funds"* into your favorite search engine.

For more information on Index Funds see pages 185-187 in the Appendix.

TIP 3. Profit from the trendy gadgets that other people are buying – Most frugal millionaires don't immediately buy all the trendy new gadgets that you see all celebrities using. Do you think those celebrities actually paid for those toys? NOT. A. CHANCE.

Marketers do want you to pay dearly for this new stuff however. How can you possibly be cool without them? Frugal millionaires wait until the gadgets become more mainstream (and less expensive) and then buy them only if they provide real value.

Frugal millionaires also do something that you might not expect when it comes to trendy gadgets. They look at the all the products that people are buying and talking about and they invest in the companies that make them. Then they can buy some of these gadgets with the profits they make. It's like investing in the company and getting the product later, for free.

When I guest lecture at universities I ask how many students have an iPhone, iPod, iPad, iMac or iWhatever, etc. Almost all of them raise their hands. Then I ask how many of them have Apple (AAPL) stock. A few people out of a hundred might raise their hands...but the look on their face usually tells me that they are raising their hands just so they will look smart!

From the example on page 151 you saw how buying Apple stock instead of Apple products during the Great Recession could have been very lucrative. You could have bought new iPads all day with the profits from investing in Apple stock.

To find out what trendy gadgets people are into these days look at what all your friends are buying, or go to these top sites to check out the latest: news.cnet.com/crave, crunchgear.com, engadget.com, gizmodo.com, and wired.com/gadgetlab.

TIP 4. Invest in real estate and use mortgages intelligently – Frugal millionaires don't like being too much in debt. They've never liked it...even before they were millionaires. And they hate paying interest. They do consider mortgages to be "good" debt however.

When you are ready, owning real estate still creates wealth, but only if done correctly. It just takes a lot longer than it used to. Why? The real estate market has been going through a huge reset that may continue for some time in many markets, and that has created opportunities for many frugal millionaires. Owning real estate should be part of a smart plan. It has to fit into your overall financial strategy.

Millennials and frugal millionaires see eye-to-eye on buying homes. Like the frugal millionaires, Millennials aren't into the big, over done McMansions according to The Wall Street Journal Real Estate Blog. Search for *"no mcmansions for millennials"* on blogs.wsj.com/developments.

The days of big castles are now mostly over, for many good reasons. So do what the frugal millionaires have always done: get the smallest mortgage, and most reasonably sized house you possibly can. Use only 15 or 30 year fixed mortgages (the shorter the better). They are very predictable. The days of Adjustable Rate Mortgages and Interest Only loans for new home and real estate investors should be long gone.

Pay off your home mortgage as quickly as you can and be done with it. Forget about the federal tax deduction for home interest...it's really dumb that people think getting a tax break on 20-30% of what their total interest expenses are each year is a good deal. Like I've been saying through this entire book: You have to stop listening to all the *often-repeated myths* people keep saying without thinking about it. You can't write-off all your mortgage interest. In simple terms you can only write off a portion of the interest you paid that, on a rough scale, is equal to your tax rate times the total interest you paid.

> MORTGAGE INTEREST WRITE-OFF EXAMPLE: If you have $10,000 in mortgage interest this year and you are in a 25% tax bracket, and you itemize your deductions and jump through a bunch of other tax hoops, you might get $2,500 deduction for that $10,000 in interest you paid. Why everyone thinks this is a great deal I have no idea. It sure makes a lot of bankers rich.

Realize that your primary home is more of a place to live than an investment while you are in it, and if you own any other real estate as a true investment it has to be positive income producing.

Why isn't your home an investment?

For those that think buying a home will be an "investment" consider this scenario: When you go to sell your house you pay a real estate commission of 6%. In the state and county where I live in there are also transfer taxes and fees that amount to another 3-4% of the total sales amount. That means it costs you approximately 10% to liquidate your "investment." If I wanted to sell $250,000 worth of stock and my financial advisor said it would cost 10% (= $25,000) in commissions and fees I would rightly go bezerk! That's insane, but it's what you will pay to sell your home "investment." Do you still think that your primary residence is an "investment"? And don't forget to add in the maintenance and repairs required to maintain the value of the home. It all adds up, so just consider it a place to live.

For real estate that would be rented out, work your financial model so that the rental income can cover the mortgage, taxes, insurance and all related expenses. Let the renters pay that mortgage off for you. You'll get some tax help with mortgage interest and depreciation deductions, etc. It's too complicated to go into here, just make sure that you have an accountant run the numbers *before* you make any rental real estate purchases.

TIP 5. Use mortgage prepayment plans to save a lot of money – Mortgages can help you get your own economic machine up and running when you are younger, but being constantly leveraged is not a lifelong mind-set for frugal millionaires.

Before you get a mortgage take a close look at the total interest you pay over the life of the loan. You will be astonished! Then you'll know why frugal millionaires dislike debt so much!

Interest on a home mortgage can be almost as much as what you borrowed (at 2011 rates). Here's an example calculated using an online mortgage interest rate tool:

House Cost:	$240,000
Down Payment:	$40,000
Mortgage Amount:	$200,000
Interest Rate:	4.5%
Mortgage Duration:	30 year fixed
Total Interest:	$164,813.42
Total Principle:	$200,000.00
Total P + I:	$364,813.42

A higher, more typical 7% loan using the same above model would yield $275,434.46 in interest payments alone. That's *more* than the principle. For more information type: "*mortgage interest calculators*" into your favorite search engine.

The solution?

You can payoff your mortgage faster by using a simple mortgage pre-payment plan. As is true with anything easy and that actually works, scammers have jumped in and taken that simple concept and made it more complicated. As a result they will find ways to make a bunch of money off you. A good rule of thumb is that if it sounds complicated, then don't do it.

There is a truly simple way to pay off your mortgage faster. If you have a new 30-year mortgage, without a pre-payment penalty, you can make a half payment every two weeks and save a lot of interest charges. Those payments will add up to 26 half payments or 13 full payments a year.

> A SIMPLE MATH EXAMPLE: Let's say you have a $1,000 monthly mortgage payment. That's $12,000 a year. If you make a half payment of $500 every two weeks, that equals 26 half payments. That's $13,000, or one additional monthly payment a year. That $1,000 goes directly to principal reduction.

Notice that by making a half payment every other week as part of a structured plan you are simply making one extra payment each year. Or, you can just make an extra full payment sometime during the year, but that seems difficult for some people to pull off. Either way, that additional payment each year can knock years off of the remaining time of your mortgage because it reduces the outstanding principal. That concept is the real "magic" that saves you a lot in interest charges. For more information type: "*mortgage prepayment*" into your favorite search engine.

> A REAL MATH EXAMPLE: Here's another example based on the scenario involving the $240,000 home from above. Let's say you put that $40,000 down and finance $200,000 @ 7% over 30 years. I used 7% because that may be a more realistic interest rate by the time you are ready to buy a home. By making a half payment every two weeks you will knock off over 5 years of payments and save over $69,000 in interest charges. That's almost 25% of your total interest payments. That's a lot of money. You can probably think of other investments to make with that extra money.

The sooner you pay off the total loan the less mortgage interest you will pay, and the more you have to invest in other opportunities. See for yourself at: mortgagecalculator.org, that's the site I used to do the above calculations.

I'll also add here that you can do the extra payment model and still work to pay off the mortgage even faster by making additional principal reduction payments over time. Once you have the "no more mortgage payments" feeling you may never go back.

TIP 6. Buy used cars, and avoid leasing and zero interest loans – Frugal millionaires love it when someone else buys a new car. That means they can acquire it two or three years later for a fraction of the price that the first owner paid. They like getting an affordable deal on a great, efficient car and they let someone else eat all the big up-front depreciation. They typically pay cash, keep it well maintained and drive it for a long time. Pretty smart, eh? Even if you can't pay cash a used car is still a smart way to go.

There are plenty of great used cars out there. Autotrader.com, Autobase.com, Cars.com and eBayMotors.com are good online sources. They will direct you to new car dealers, used car dealers and private owners. Kelley Blue Book (KBB.com) and Edmunds.com can provide good research. There are others, but start with the above.

People turn in their cars all the time, and for various reasons. Some people do short term leases, dumb for them...but good for you, and others just get bored with their cars. There are plenty of good deals out there.

Here are some used car buying tips:

> **- Consider the total cost of ownership.** The cost of a good used car is one thing. The costs of maintenance, repairs, insurance, fuel, etc., are another. If you've saved up money for a good used car and spend all of that money on the car you might be in for some additional financial surprises down the road.

> **- Know your numbers before you get ready to negotiate.** Big depreciation = Big lost money. Cars typically depreciate 40% every three years. Some are lower and some are higher. All but a few manufacturers can claim their models have good resale value. Be armed with data to make your case when you negotiate a used car price with a dealer. A car that originally sold for $40,000 new would, on average, be worth around $24,000 after three years. The first three years represent the biggest chunk of depreciation in terms of actual dollars. Let someone else foot the bill for that. At the end of 6 years that same car would depreciate

another 40% off the 3rd year value. It would then be worth $14,400.

Run the numbers from Kelley Blue Book on certified pre-owned, retail, and private party values to help you negotiate. It will give you an idea of the range of pricing for the used car you are interested in. These prices are not set in stone. Everything is negotiable, up to a point.

- Get a car with remaining factory warranty and consider additional warranties. Try to buy a car with at least one year's worth of warranty left. This is a must. But don't buy the first few years of production of a newer model used car or the first few years of a new engine type. As hard as they try to make perfect cars, the manufacturers still have to get some of the bugs out on the assembly line over time.

Many cars today come with 6 to 10 year factory warranties. The annual mileage allowed isn't all that high (10K-12K miles) but these types of cars can be great purchases right after college. If you buy them with low miles at the "3-year-old" mark you will still have a lot of warranty left.

Also consider getting an extended warranty. Most of the consumer agencies say not to buy them. Do whatever makes you comfortable with an extended warranty, but do your research on the durability of the car you are interested in before you get to the dealership. Don't be sold by the finance person once you get there. Extended warranties are very high profit for dealers - so there is room for negotiating. One additional note: Extended warranties generally aren't as comprehensive and the original factory warranty.

- Consider "certified pre-owned" car. Cars that have "certified pre-owned" warranties (called CPO or similar names) are often a great deal for used car buyers. They offer an additional warranty by a year or two. Dealers charge a premium for these cars because they have to inspect, refurbish and warranty them. The premium charged is usually more than the associated costs so consider that a good place to negotiate on the final car price. The CPO warranty may not be a full "bumper-to-bumper" version that the car had when it was new... it's typically just a "mechanical" warranty. They are certainly worth looking at.

- Find out what current owners think. If you've locked on to a car that you are interested in go to the Internet and find the owner and enthusiast blogs. If you really want to know what's going on with that particular car model as far as praises, faults, reliability, problems, recalls, and all the other pluses and minuses the blogs are a great place to get info.

Current owners don't hold back in their opinions if their cars are having troubles...especially when they are hiding behind an online alias. You might find that you are getting a great car or about to purchase a money pit. If you uncover major defects that are repairable make sure you find out if the work has been done before you buy the car. This may also help you in your decision to get an extended warranty.

- Got receipts? When you are buying a used car always ask for receipts and any paperwork that the previous owner has. Many dealers track the car's service history on their computers through its Vehicle Identification Number (VIN). All cars need service. That includes: minor and major services, oil and fluid changes, tire rotations, wheel alignment, radiator flushes, and brake fluid flushes, etc. If you are looking at a 3-year-old used car it probably should have had, at least: oil changes, tire rotations, a brake fluid flush and possibly a minor service. If the current owner can't seem to find the receipts and a dealer can't confirm the services I would seriously think twice about buying the car.

- Invest in a CARFAX. Many auto body shops are doing fantastic work these days. They can make cars look brand new after minor and major accidents. You probably would still like to know if the car has had a reported repair, right? It's hard to avoid finding a car that hasn't been slightly damaged in some way or another. It should rarely be a "deal killer" on making a purchase if the work is disclosed and of high quality. That's why investing in a CARFAX is so important.

Car buying sites like Autotrader.com often include a free CARFAX report as part of their resources for buyers. You can also buy the reports on the CARFAX website. The VIN# of the car you are interested in is all you need to get the information on CARFAX. Current pricing offers include a single report purchase or a 5-pack purchase. It's not much more money for the 5-pack version. If you have a few friends who are also in the market for used cars then why not consider sharing a 5-pack? (Most of you are already doing this kind of sharing on Netflix, right?)

ADDITIONAL THOUGHTS WORTH DISCUSSING:

Are leases a good idea?

- Leases promote over-consumption. Leases look like a good deal because they can "put you into more car than you could actually afford to buy" (or so the sales speak says...), but they actually promote over-consumption. They are really a bad idea, in my humble opinion. You never own the car and you have to keep leasing one to keep driving. That means you keep making car payments...forever. Constantly making car payments is not a way to build your financial future. Not surprisingly, car dealers and finance companies love lease customers!

- Let the lessee eat the "new car" depreciation. Frugal millionaires love leases, but not because they are doing the leasing. It's because they can buy the car inexpensively after its been returned by the original lessee.

- Turn it in with the exact mileage allowance – or pay dearly. I leased a car once and regretted it. It's agonizing to have to wonder if you are going to go over your lease mileage allowance. The "per mile" overage fees can be huge especially if you misjudged the number of miles you were going to drive annually. The only way you get what you *overpay* for (*sarcasm added*) is if you turn the car in with exactly the number of miles you contracted for. If you are over the miles you pay a penalty, if you are under the miles you have overpaid for the lease. It's hard to win at the leasing game.

- But I can write it off! People use every excuse to justify a lease for business purposes. "I can write it off!" is my favorite. Did you know that you can also write off a regular car payment for business too? And those payments are typically lower. It's not that difficult. The only real difference between writing off a leased car and one bought on installment payments is that sales taxes are paid monthly on a lease and paid in-full up-front on a car purchase.

People tend to parrot back whatever *often-repeated myth* a salesperson or leasing agent says to them, especially if it helps justify the emotional purchase decision they just made...the above is a good case in point.

- Your car insurance will probably be more expensive. When it comes to car insurance, chances are good that leasing a car will cost you more in premiums than if you bought it. If you are young with a minimal credit history and you lease, that's a big signal to your insurance company that your credit might be minimal, or not good. If it were good you would have probably bought the car on a credit based payment plan. Insurance companies, like banks and other lenders, like people with good credit histories.

The only reason *to* lease a car, and it's a slim one at best, is if you have money to burn and you want to "own" some exotic brand for a very limited period of time. Chances are if it's truly exotic, it's probably better to buy it and resell it at a profit later. But I'm not a huge fan of that scenario either.

Bottom Line: Leases are for financial fools...feel free to quote me on that.

What about "zero interest" new car loans?

They sound great, right? No big interest payments – Whoo-Hooo! But you are still buying a new car that will depreciate heavily in the first 3-4 years of its life. It's the same 40% depreciation model that was mentioned previously...and guess who eats all that? You do!

Why do I have zero interest in zero interest loans?

Let's say that you buy a new $25,000 car with a zero interest rate deal. In 4 years that car will be worth about $12,500. While there was no interest fee, that new car depreciated at a rate of over $3,000 a year. If you bought a four-year-old version of that car for $12,500 and financed it at 7% over three years your total finance charges would be around $1,400. Your total cost would be about $13,900 and you would own the car outright after you've paid it off. You'd still be paying for that new car in the "zero interest rate" loan scenario. The simple math is: $25,000 - $13,900 = money you wasted.

Isn't resale value important?

Here's another one of those *often-repeated myths*: You need to buy a car with high resale value. Not true. The car manufacturers want you to think that's important because they want you to keep flipping over to a new car every 3-4 years. If you are smart with your car purchase you will own it for a long time and resale value will become irrelevant or at least immaterial by the time you sell it. Given the quality of most cars today the chances of getting a "lemon" are quite low.

Some cars that have high resale value and high reliability are in demand. Buying a two to three year old car with high resale value probably won't make sense because the cost difference between new and used is very small. Car dealers charge higher used car prices for these types of cars on their car lots to try to help justify the sticker prices of the new cars they sell. If that's the case find another brand of used car to buy. And keep driving it for a long time.

~

Cars are better made every year, but most people treat them like fashion statements or disposable appliances. Whatever kind of used car you buy, take care of it and have fun with it. Drive it for as long as possible. That's how you win at the car buying game.

TIP 7. Use the perks and convenience part of a credit card, but not the credit part – Frugal millionaires know how to leverage the credit card companies perfectly. They have as few credit cards as possible. That's usually one credit card for personal use and one for business use; and each with big credit limits that they never use more than 30% of. They will also first job ~ first paycheck

have debit cards tied to their checking or savings accounts. All these combined resources provide more than enough cash and credit availability for them.

They pay off the credit cards every month. They never pay an interest charge but they get all the conveniences and perks. They don't like the "credit" part, but they do love the "card" part. They treat the card like they are using cash, and they don't part with their cash without a really good reason.

As I noted in the previous chapter, some of you will say, "Of course they pay the cards off every month...they are millionaires!" There's another example of those *often-repeated myths* popping up again. They've actually always paid their credit cards off – since the beginning, since before they were millionaires. They have learned to never over-extend themselves. Credit card debt is one of the fastest ways to get into a financial rat-hole. Follow the simple rule that if you never pay credit card interest, you can't get yourself in trouble.

~

So that's how the frugal millionaires do it. And they've got the bank accounts to prove it. Listen to what they have to say and pay attention to how they operate. You didn't see anything underhanded or unethical did you? And you're probably surprised by that. The assumptions are that most millionaires did something sneaky to get where they are financially. That's not true for the 70 that I spoke to. You wouldn't even recognize them if they were standing next to you. They are just regular, smart people, and they are a lot like you. They just got a head start. Now you have one too.

~~~

DID YOU HEAR THIS IN HIGH SCHOOL?

~

I was a guest speaker at a National Honor Society induction ceremony in Florida a few years ago. As you would expect, all the students being inducted were bright, ambitious and leaders in their high school and community. They were each going to go far in life. I told them that as they embarked on their college careers, and ultimately their life careers, they should keep this thought in mind:

> *Make sure that the career you are interested in can pay for the education you're about to get and the lifestyle you want to live after you graduate college.*

The parents all smiled and nodded in agreement, but many of the students seemed puzzled by what I was saying. Why? Because they had no concept of what certain careers paid and what their college bills might add up to. They probably just thought it would all take care of itself. Really? People still think this way? Oh yes, they do.

Here's the Advanced Placement version that everyone in high school (who is college bound, at least) should think about:

1. Research the short-term and long-term demand for the career that you are interested in.
2. Find out what schools have the major that you are interested in, and check out as many of them as you can. (That's assuming you even know at this point in your life.)
3. Determine what the full costs of your education might be, including student loan interest, etc.

4. Understand what your earning potential will be for the career you are interested in.
5. Then ask yourself if the career you want can pay for the education you are about to get and your future lifestyle.

I'm not one for being a dream-buster but I am one for being realistic. Those honor students surely hadn't thought about whether their future career would be able to pay for their education bills and the lifestyle they wanted. And, for some reason their parents were agreeing with me, but still shielding their kids from reality. Was this a big case of denial? Maybe. And what about all the students who weren't honor students? How would they be dealing with these same issues?

After the ceremony I wondered: Why couldn't the parents have told these students what I just had? If they already had maybe the students wouldn't have seemed so puzzled. Would it make the students unhappy if their parents asked them to be realistic in their college and career choices? Telling them would have been the right thing to do.

Why? Let's say that one of these honor students wanted to follow their dreams of being an art major. (By the way, I loved my art classes in college.) That student would initially be making $33,500 a year according to CBSMoneywatch.com, and that is assuming they could get a job in their field. They would be paying between $40K for a public university or $100K for a private university education to even be considered for that new job.

Would that be worth it or would their dreams need to be more realistic and practical before they decided on their major? Did their parents not have any idea about how to talk about the college costs, careers and money with their children? I suspected that "all of the above" might be the answer. It's hard when you want the best for your kids, and talking about the real world can be difficult.

The most important advice I could ever offer to high school students is to find the best college/university that they can afford, and one that matches their educational needs. It's the student's life, not their parents. Attending an expensive private or Ivy League school doesn't really help much if the student is miserable, "in over their head" academically, or just as employable as any other student upon graduation, just so their parents could boast about the school they were going to. If the student is unsure, he or she should try a community college first to get an idea of what's interesting to them before spending a lot of time and money getting educated. There's no shame in that at all. It's actually very smart.

I learned a long time ago that 95% of the time, the education you get and how you apply yourself, is more important than the school you went to. Some parents don't always get that. Not to mention that having student loan debt that's massive may not be the best way to start off your working career, especially these days.

According to CNNMoney.com the average student debt for 2010 was $24,000 and up 6% from the previous year. The range was $13,000 to $30,000. The data came from a report entitled: *The Project on Student Debt.*

Consider this *2010-2011 College Salary Report* data from Payscale.com.

Here are the TOP 15 Undergraduate College Degrees by Salary:

	Starting Median Pay
1. Petroleum Engineering	$93,000
2. Chemical Engineering	$64,800
3. Nuclear Engineering	$63,900
4. Computer Engineering	$61,200
5. Electrical Engineering	$60,800
6. Aerospace Engineering (tie)	$59,400

6. Materials & Science Engineering (tie)	$59,400
7. Mechanical Engineering	$58,300
8. Industrial Engineering	$58,200
9. Software Engineering	$56,700
10. Applied Mathematics	$56,400
11. Computer Science	$56,200
12. Biomedical Engineering	$54,800
13. Civil Engineering	$53,500
14. Building Construction	$52,900
15. Management Info Systems	$50,900

(I guess I should have been an engineering major.)

Here are the BOTTOM 15 Undergraduate College Degrees by Salary (starting with the lowest):

	Starting Median Pay
1. Child and Family Studies	$29,500
2. Elementary Education	$31,600
3. Social Work	$31,800
4. Athletic Training (tie)	$32,800
4. Exercise Science (tie)	$32,800
5. Recreational Leisure Studies	$33,300
6. Art	$33,500
7. Interior Design	$34,400
8. Religious Studies (tie)	$34,700
8. Theology (tie)	$34,700
9. Horticulture	$35,000
10. Paralegal Studies/Law	$35,100
11. Graphic Design	$35,400
12. Criminal Justice (tie)	$35,600
12. Interdisciplinary Studies (tie)	$35,600
13. Culinary Arts	$35,900
14. Special Education	$36,000
15. Music	$36,700

NOTE: These are starting job salaries. Salary performance of these jobs over 5, 10 and 15 year periods wasn't covered in this study. If you are in the top 2% of all earners in your job category then the sky is usually the limit on your success rate...relatively speaking. But what about the other 98% of us looking for those jobs? That's where the majority of us will fall.

So here's a thought:

Sometimes you have to separate what your career
passion could be, from what your life passion is.
If they can be combined and pay for your education
and lifestyle then that's great,
but it doesn't always work out that way.

Maybe that's why so many wealthy people (doctors, lawyers, business people, etc.) support the arts but aren't artists for a living?

It's great to have dreams, it's even greater to do your very best, be realistic, and actually accomplish something. I tell high school students to think about what they want to do in life, how much it will cost to get there, and if they can afford to pay for it along with their lifestyle after they graduate. And think about it as far in advance as possible. Can they separate their life career from their life passion and still be happy? If yes, then they should find an affordable way to make it happen without getting massively in debt.

Do those younger than you a big favor. Get them thinking about these things while they are in high school, or before they declare a major in college. Very few students younger than you are thinking about these things right now. You could make a big difference in someone else's life by telling them these things now.

~~~

FINAL THOUGHTS ON
MONEY & LIFE

~

Why do millionaires get advantages in life that others don't? They *make* those advantages happen for themselves. There is a certain level of confidence that you just "have" when you've got a cushion of money in the bank and you know that you can take some risks and still survive your mistakes. Everyone makes mistakes. It's how quickly you recover and learn from them that will make the difference. If you are living paycheck-to-paycheck it makes it that much more difficult.

I've pushed you hard about having financial goals and a plan, getting that Emergency Fund set up and saving as much as you can so you can finally start investing someday. I want you to have that "millionaire feeling" of safety and security even if you aren't a millionaire...yet. I will warn you that it's contagious, and once you've caught the desire to control your financial destiny, with no excuses, your life will change forever.

I've also been relentless with you about not succumbing to the *often-repeated myths* about money, jobs and life. How did I do on that? Many of my successes in life have come from *not* doing what everyone else is doing. Hopefully you heard me say: Never invest more than you can afford to lose, and: Always live below your means. These are simple concepts that most people find impossible to execute on. These are just some of the ideas that you can use to be more successful in life and increase your net worth.

No one really knows the exact timing on when you will have truly "made it" financially and in your career. Maybe that's never supposed to fully happen. Maybe you're just supposed to enjoy the journey because we never know when exactly it will end. Regardless of that, having the Emergency Fund and savings accounts will make a world of difference to your stress levels. And sometime in the future your financial plan may yield returns that will tell you your money is working harder for you than you are for it. That will be a great day.

When you control your financial destiny all kinds of doors open up for you. Once you pay off all your debts you can be your own banker without all the annoying forms to fill out and hoops to jump through every time you want to get a personal or business loan. You will have flexibility to move quickly when great opportunities are presented to you.

One big theme in this book that is readily visible in all the ideas you've read is the concept of personal responsibility. You cannot achieve any of what I've just shared with you if you don't accept personal responsibility for your actions, financially or otherwise.

I have a theory that I came up with years ago that has yet to be disproved. It goes like this:

"95% of the time people create their own S#!T storms!"

And I'm being generous on the 95%...it's more like 99%. What I mean by that quote is most of the time we create our own problems because of the decisions we make. But being modern humans we are often very good at finding something or someone else to blame for why *we* can't make the right choices. Be conscious of that and work actively to not make those *"S#!T storms"* part of your world. Just doing that alone can allow you to accomplish great things. Admitting that you have done something wrong and growing because of it is truly a positive learning experience.

Take control of everything you can in your life now. You worked hard to get where you are...and there are more great things to come. It will be different from what college was. No one else will do it for you. No one will care about your job or money more than you do. Very few people will cut you slack when you get it wrong or allow you to make excuses.

Your relationship with your job and money, just like with people who are important to you, needs to be constantly cared for. You can do it but you have to be actively involved in the process. You now have more than enough information and ideas to help you get started.

Building a financial empire, even a small one, takes time and patience. Enjoy where you are in the process right now. Don't rush yourself. As long as you know where you are going and taking steps to get there you will be fine, and you will be better off than the majority of the population.

My hope is that as you get older you will have great successes in your life. But know that while success isn't always about money, it sure helps.

One recent graduate that I have mentioned a few times in the book recently e-mailed these thoughts to me:

"Many people think that the more money you make the more you want to buy. But that's not why I am driven. I want freedom. I want to be financially free to live a life of exploration, innovation and learning. I want to be free with my time and be able to provide a certain lifestyle for my family and be able to give back generously to others, especially young people."

I can tell you that he's well on his way. We should all strive to be like that.

Now is your time. You will never get this part of your life back. Be smart about your career and money now and you will have less to worry about in the future...a lot less. If you use some of the ideas in this book to help get there, I'll know I did my part to help you. Nothing would make me happier.

Good Luck!

Jeff Lehman
Seattle, WA

Appendix:
More on Index Funds

~

Index Funds are very popular with smart investors and they come in many flavors. Over the past few years the financial marketplace has offered so many "Index Fund" products that it can get confusing. A pure Index Fund has lower transaction costs because it tracks to a benchmark index (like the S&P 500) and is automated – which means the stocks in the mix are passively rebalanced on a set schedule. These are my favorite type of Index Funds. (*Passive rebalancing* means that as the companies that make up an index have different market values over time, and/or as those companies in the index also change over time, so does the value and make up of the fund. It is automatically recalculated on a set schedule.)

According to my financial advisor the confusing part is that indexes are just packaging methodologies for creating a fund. Mutual Funds and Exchange Traded Funds (ETFs) then are simply ways for investors to buy those methodologies and diversify their investments. But since there are virtually an unlimited number of company combinations, there are literally thousands of funds to choose from.

Where it gets really confusing – if not totally maddening – is when financial companies refer to their product offerings somewhat interchangeably. You can have Index Funds that are Mutual Funds, and Index Funds that are ETFs, etc. And everyone, it seems, has an interpretation of how they all should be categorized. Confused yet?

Additionally, there are two ways to manage a fund: passively or actively.

As noted above, when a fund is automated and tracks to a benchmark index it is passively managed.

Anytime a methodology is created regarding what stocks are in a fund, and in what quantities (also known as "weightings"), that is considered an actively managed fund. These funds supposedly have smart money managers behind them making the decisions – and that costs more in management fees. This, of course, explains why actively managed funds typically under-perform a market index and make their managers wealthy *(sarcasm added)*. If these funds do over-perform, money quickly flows into them and they don't typically continue to perform as well as they have historically. There are very few exceptions.

The basic difference between most funds comes down to: the methodologies (what's in the fund), sales charges, expense ratio (the cost of managing the fund) and exactly how they are managed.

A pure Index Fund keeps costs low and investing simple. Fortunately, low cost and simple is good for you the consumer, but not always good for Wall Street profits (unless their funds can attract a lot of business). As pure Index Funds have grown more popular and attracted smart investors the financial institutions have started packaging up all sorts of Index Funds that sound a lot like pure Index Funds. They generally aren't (by my definition anyway), because they don't track a particular benchmark index.

Also - when new funds are created, financial institutions can often confuse the terms and that can confuse you. Why all the confusion? They want your money. Confused customers need more guidance and can be steered in the direction the financial institution wants to steer you in – meaning right towards a particular product offering. You have to be a savvy investor and really know when your advisor is talking apples-to-apples or apples-to-oranges.

You can have multiple S&P 500 Index Funds. Here are examples of two: a S&P 500 *Market Weight* Index Fund and a S&P 500 *Equal Weight* Index Fund. They sound similar, but they are different:

MARKET WEIGHT INDEX FUNDS – If Apple Computer (AAPL) has a market capitalization (= total market value of the company) equal to 2.5% of the total value of all the S&P 500 companies then that's the amount of Apple stock the *Market Weight* Index Fund would contain. Therefore, if a particular *Market Weight* Index Fund is valued at $100,000,000 then 2.5% of the dollars in the fund are in Apple (AAPL) stock.

EQUAL WEIGHT INDEX FUNDS – If the Index Fund were an *Equal Weight* fund then $1/500^{th}$ of the fund dollars (because there are 500 companies in the S&P 500) would be in Apple stock. Every other stock in the index would also be $1/500^{th}$ of the fund regardless of the company's market capitalization.

See the difference? They are both viable options, but in my mind the most precise S&P 500 Index Fund is the *Market Weight* version, even though it favors the bigger companies in the benchmark index rather than the smaller ones. Those companies got big for a reason after all.

Not all *Market or Equal Weight* Index Funds have the same cost and expense structures. You should only be interested in no-load (no up-front commissions) and low expense ratio pure Index Funds. Make sure that you take note of their investment minimums and procedures. How you buy them also matters. Buying into a pure Index Fund that is mutual fund based typically carries no transaction fees and can be bought in small amounts – which is great for the small investor. Buying into an Index Fund that is ETF based can be just like buying a stock, and that usually means a transaction fee. That's not good if you are buying small amounts with each paycheck.

As always, consult your written financial plan and goals and talk to a financial advisor before making any investments. Only consider this form of investment when you have financial stability and money to invest.

I apologize for going on and on here, but I wanted to make this investment option more clear for you and I certainly didn't want to spend more time talking about engagement rings than Index Funds!

~~~

Recommended Reading List

Personal Finance Books

Don't Sweat the Small Stuff about Money, Richard Carlson,
Hyperion, ISBN: 0-7868-8637-4

The Little Book of Common Sense Investing, John C. Bogle,
Wiley, ISBN: 978-0-470-10210-7

The New Coffeehouse Investor, Bill Schultheis,
Portfolio, ISBN: 159184245X

The Total Money Makeover, Dave Ramsay,
Thomas Nelson, ISBN: 978-0-7852-8908-1

The Ten Commandments of Money, Liz Weston,
Hudson Street Press, ISBN: 978-1594630743

The Frugal Millionaires, Jeff Lehman,
Mentor Press LLC, ISBN: 978-0-9768999-2-1
(Did you think I wouldn't recommend this one?)

Stop Acting Rich...and start living like a real millionaire
Thomas J. Stanley, PhD, Wiley, ISBN: 978-1-118-01157-7

Life Books

Simplify Your Life, Elaine St. James,
Hyperion, ISBN: 0-7868-6411-7

From College to Career, Lindsey Pollak,
Collins, ISBN: 978-0-06-114259-8

Acknowledgements

Special Thanks To My Advisory Crew

Tony daRoza – Managing Director – Investments
Merrill Lynch Wealth Management

Jennifer Thomsen – Financial Advisor
MassMutual Financial Group

Michael Hagy – Financial Advisor – AXA Advisors

George Andrade – Financial Advisor – Edward Jones

Jon Lehman – Associate Dean
Vanderbilt University
Owen Graduate School of Management

Karl Sooder – Professor
University of Central Florida – College of Business

Jack Rhodes – Professor
University of Washington – Foster School of Business

John Durham – Professor
University of San Francisco
CEO, Managing General Partner
Catalyst S+F

Todd Heckel – Technology Executive
Adobe Systems, Inc.

Ryan Michael Scott – Design Consultant

Christine Willmsen – Editor

Rick Van Ness – Financial Author

About the Author

Jeff Lehman is an award-winning author. This is his third book. He is also an entrepreneur, consultant, mentor, former print and Internet media executive, life long sailor and occasional stand-up comedian. He is an alumnus of the University of Central Florida (BSBA, MBA) and has been inducted into the UCF College of Business Hall of Fame. He mentors business students from UCF, the University of Washington, and other universities. He has also studied architecture and law. Profits from his books are donated to selected charities.

Jeff currently lives in Seattle, WA and can be reached at:
www.FirstJobFirstPaycheck.com

To share your successes and ideas go to:
Facebook.com/FirstJobFirstPaycheck

More award-winning books from Jeff:

The Sales Manager's Mentor, 3rd Edition
Mentor Press LLC, ISBN# 978-0-9768999-7-6

The Frugal Millionaires
Mentor Press LLC, ISBN# 978-0-9768999-2-1